Lit...

Peter Robinson became a Buddhist monk at the age of forty-five. As Phra Peter Pannapadipo, he founded the Students' Education Trust – a charity to help impoverished students and novice monks continue their higher education. Monks cannot earn money or directly fundraise, so after ten years Phra Peter temporarily disrobed from the monkhood to establish SET as a Foundation in Thailand.

ALSO BY PHRA PETER PANNAPADIPO

Phra Farang

LITTLE ANGELS

PHRA PETER PANNAPADIPO

arrow books

First published in the United Kingdom by Arrow Books in 2005

1 3 5 7 9 10 8 6 4 2

This edition first published in 2001 by Post Books,
the publishing arm of the *Bangkok Post*

Arrow Books
The Random House Group Limited
20 Vauxhall Bridge Road, London, SW1V 2SA

Random House Australia (Pty) Limited
20 Alfred Street, Milsons Point, Sydney,
New South Wales 2061, Australia

Random House New Zealand Limited
18 Poland Road, Glenfield
Auckland 10, New Zealand

Random House (Pty) Limited
Endulini, 5a Jubilee Road, Parktown 2193, South Africa

The Random House Group Limited Reg. No. 954009

www.randomhouse.co.uk

A CIP catalogue record for this book
is available from the British Library

Papers used by Random House
are natural, recyclable products made from wood grown in
sustainable forests. The manufacturing processes conform to
the environmental regulations of the country of origin

ISBN 0 09 948448 X

Typeset by Palimpsest Book Production Limited
Polmont, Stirlingshire
Printed and bound in Great Britain by
Bookmarque Ltd, Croydon, Surrey

Introduction

According to official figures, in the year 2000 there were 97,875 Buddhist novice monks in Thailand. That figure had increased from five years previously, when it stood at 87,686. If those figures referred to any other monastic order, it might be superficially concluded that there had been a gradual increase in the number of young men drawn to the religious, spiritual or reclusive life. To a Buddhist that would be encouraging, if true, but it's most unlikely to be the case in Thailand. The increase is more likely an indication of the continuing poverty and lack of opportunity amongst many already disadvantaged Thai families, especially in rural areas, and is a sad reflection of the parents' inability to care for and educate their children. In Thailand, young boys frequently become novice monks simply because their impoverished parents can't afford to feed them, clothe them or send them to school. There is nowhere else for them to go except to a monastery. For many boys, ordaining and studying at a free monastic high school is the only way they can complete their secular education. The increasing number of novice monks may also be an equally sad reflection of the failure of successive Thai governments to properly prepare the country's poorest young people for the future, or to ensure they have the educational opportunities and practical skills they deserve and which the country needs.

Despite these opening comments, *Little Angels* is not a social research document, nor is it a scholarly, in-depth survey into the lives of novice monks in present-day Thailand. Neither is it a book about Buddhism, at least not as a philosophy or religion. Rather, it presents one aspect of the human face of Buddhism in Thailand, of which there are many. The book simply relates the stories of twelve young men – some of them no more than little boys – who all, because of their circumstances, now wear the robes of the Buddhist novice monk.

I'm not going to draw any conclusions from the stories featured here. It would be unrealistic to generalise or theorise about all the novices in Thailand from such a small sampling. However, even from these twelve stories, some overall conclusions are inevitable and obvious. None of the boys seem to harbour any great regrets about having become novices, even though it was often not a voluntary choice, nor even a willing one. Some, although initially reluctant to ordain, acknowledge in retrospect that it was the best thing that could have happened to them, considering their circumstances at the time. Most also appreciate that what they have learned whilst wearing the robes will be of value to them in later life. Living as novices, trying to follow their precepts and learning the *Dhamma*, the Buddha's teaching, has given them a moral and ethical framework around which they will be able to build their lives as laymen after they disrobe. Most of the boys also acknowledge that if they hadn't ordained, they would have been unlikely to further their secular education beyond primary level. Without the important diploma proving six years of high school study, many might have faced quite bleak and unsatisfactory futures; working in the paddy fields, labouring on city building sites or in other mundane, dead-end jobs. Living in monasteries may even have protected some of the boys from the temptations and dangers faced by young people in modern Thailand, particularly from amphetamine (speed) abuse. These very positive results of novice ordination for boys from impoverished backgrounds should be acknowledged.

Although the novices featured in the book seem grateful for the opportunities that ordaining has given them, it is clear that most look forward to disrobing. Whilst they do not necessarily dislike the life and try hard to fit into their role, ordaining was often the only option for themselves and their parents. Because of their backgrounds and lack of alternatives, some feel trapped in the robes. The role they have to play is too difficult for them; the robes are too heavy. Given the opportunities to lead the life of ordinary young men outside the monastery, to study for a useful and practical qualification, to contribute to the future of their country and to be part of the real world, they would grab those opportunities eagerly.

Unfortunately, some novices may eventually take full ordination as monks when they reach age twenty simply because they can see no other more attractive or practical alternative. That may be especially true for boys who ordain as novices and then remain in their little village monasteries. Rural village monasteries usually offer few, if any, opportunities for either secular or religious education. Village monks, who theoretically should teach the novices, may themselves never have moved from their village monastery, nor had the opportunity or inclination to study. Even by the time they reach twenty and become eligible to ordain as monks, novices in rural monasteries may have learned little more than the very simplest and most popular Thai Buddhist teachings, superstitious Animist rituals, and how to chant, splash holy water about or give blessings. Often they are not required or expected to do much else by their farming communities. They may drift apathetically from being novices into becoming monks and then carry on the same relaxed, lazy and largely pointless lifestyle that they have already grown used to while in the robes. They may make no great effort to improve themselves in any way and may have little genuine interest in the life they are following, nor any real understanding of the Buddha's teaching. For many, it's a living, if nothing else.

After ordaining in their villages, other novices quickly move to town or city monasteries that offer opportunities for secular education. They often disrobe immediately after completing their six years of high school studies at the monastery schools. Knowing they can't study further, but satisfied enough just to have had a basic education, they may then return to their villages to help their families work on the land. Others look for jobs in the cities and send money home to their families. An ambitious few, if they can find the money for fees and other expenses, or are lucky enough to be offered a scholarship, may go on to acquire practical skills at technical or vocational colleges or even, in quite rare cases, degrees from secular universities.

A minority of novices undoubtedly has, or develops, a deep and genuine interest in the teaching of the Buddha and in the monastic life. After ordaining in their villages, such novices will move to larger monasteries with schools that offer good religious education, as well as a secular curriculum. They may be sufficiently inspired to want to follow and practice the Buddha's teaching for the rest of their lives, intending to ordain as monks as soon as they are old enough, and to continue their religious studies. Such novices are the future of the *Sangha*, the order of monks. Other novices may be very reluctant to wear the robes at all but, with few other options, reluctant novices may grow up to be reluctant monks. Uninterested novices may drift into being uninterested monks. Poorly educated novices will become poorly educated monks. They may not be bad monks, but without genuine commitment they will still be little more than men in saffron robes.

There are approximately 300,000 monks in Thailand. Unfortunately, the real strength of Buddhism in the country cannot be measured just by counting the number of bodies wrapped in robes, but rather by the spiritual commitment of those wearing the robes. In recent years, the lay people's respect for the Thai Sangha has been badly damaged by the inappropriate behaviour of some well-known monks. Faith in the community of monks as a whole has diminished. To become a strong, vital and respected force again, the Sangha needs to be comprised of monks who have a genuine desire to practice the Buddha's teaching, not those who wear the robes simply because they have few other alternatives, or are too lazy to seek them. But that's just the opinion of this foreign monk.

There are twelve stories here but they weren't culled from dozens more. In preparing this book, I didn't interview hundreds of novices in order to choose the dozen stories I found most interesting. I interviewed only the featured novices, plus three others. Three of the original twelve unexpectedly disrobed before their interviews were completed, so they had to be replaced. There was nothing outwardly special about any of the twelve novices and I knew little or nothing about them before the interviews started. They were chosen at random and mainly because they were easily accessible to me. They originally came from many different parts of Thailand but some had moved from province to province before eventually arriving at my own monastery in Nakhon Sawan Province, in the northern region. The province is well known for the quality of its monastic schools. With a few of those novices, I was already at least slightly acquainted. Some lived in other monasteries close to my own and I had never met them before.

Thai youngsters are generally very shy, so getting the stories out of the twelve novices was a lengthy and sometimes difficult process. First, each was given a form that asked one hundred questions, many of which were quite personal. I gave a lot of thought to drawing up the questions and tried to ensure that they covered every aspect of the novices' lives, before and after they ordained. The questions concerned their family backgrounds, their lives as children at home, their education, why they became novices, whether they were willing or reluctant to ordain, what benefits they thought they had gained from their time in the robes, how they personally practised as novices, their dreams for the future, and much more. I didn't necessarily intend to use all that information in every story but I needed it to get an overall picture of the life and character of each novice.

Few of the questions could be answered with a simple 'yes' or 'no' and most required lengthy and thoughtful answers. Some of the novices were quite young or poorly educated and found it difficult to express themselves. They received help and sympathetic encouragement from my Thai translator. None of the novices could write well in English, so they completed their forms in Thai. Their answers then had to be translated for me, since I do not read Thai. On the basis of the written and translated answers, I then formulated further questions to ask at personal interviews, aided by my translator. In some cases, the novices were interviewed several times, especially those from the most difficult backgrounds who were at first reluctant to speak openly about their personal and sometimes traumatic experiences. I then wrote the stories in English and the outline of each was explained to the novice in Thai, to ensure that each was happy with the way I had presented his story. In telling me their stories, a few of the novices mentioned incidents that they felt embarrassed or ashamed about. They asked me not to identify them too precisely so, in three stories, the name has been changed and the photograph is not of the novice featured in the story.

Sometimes, when translating from one language to another, important details or concepts may be distorted or lost altogether, but I think we got it right. My translator was a student who was then in his final year of studying for a degree in English at a local university. His English was almost fluent and, at the time, he lived in free student accommodation at my monastery as a *dek wat*, or temple boy. I chose him as the translator partly because he had previously been a novice monk for six years and had gained his high school diploma from a monastic school. He also came from a similar poor rural background to most of the novices featured. His help was of great value not just in the translations, but also in increasing my own understanding of some of the relevant social issues.

The novices' stories form the main part of the book but I have preceded them with some background about novice life generally, and some of the basic social and cultural factors involved, so that readers can more readily understand and appreciate what the novices have to say. In a few cases, when there have been significant subsequent developments in the novices' lives, I have added the details to the end of the stories. I have also included a couple of stories from Western novices, since they have a different approach to the idea of ordination from their Thai counterparts.

Some of the novices whose stories are related here have been very frank, as I asked them to be. They openly admit that their behaviour often falls far short of the novice ideal. The ideal would be difficult for any normal boy to achieve in any circumstances. The novices are just ordinary young men and adolescent boys, most of them from disadvantaged backgrounds. Some try very hard as novices and a few others don't make much effort, but most do the best they can in a very restrictive environment and in a role in which they are not always entirely comfortable.

Before I ordained as a monk, I travelled widely in areas of Thailand that few foreigners visit. I was then the director of a UK charity that worked with impoverished children in the northeast of the country and I often stayed in remote little villages. In some communities, I was the first *farang*, foreigner, the villagers had ever seen. Because of my travels and work, and since living in Thailand as a monk, I thought I had developed quite a good understanding of the country and its social problems. But I was still surprised by some of the stories the novices told me. When I first heard them, a few of the stories made me very sad; it seemed so unjust that young people suffered from such lack of opportunity. Other stories were amusing and a few were even inspiring, in a quiet sort of way. Before starting the novice interviews, I knew that all the boys would probably have come from disadvantaged rural families, so I expected the theme of poverty to be repeated often. Even so, I was appalled at how extreme it was in some cases. I was also genuinely shocked by how many of the boys had been exposed to the temptation of drugs at a very young age, or had suffered abuse at the hands of drunken and violent relatives. These were recurrent factors in the stories. But there were other recurrent factors too: of love, sacrifice and a determination by parents to give their sons a better start in life than they themselves had been given.

Although a few of the stories may seem tragic or shocking to Western readers, I haven't written this book to shock. In general terms, I doubt if the stories are particularly unusual amongst Thai novices. I am sure that similar tales could be repeated by thousands of other novices and hundreds of thousands of young people, girls as well as boys. But for the casual visitor to Thailand, staying in a luxury hotel or lying on a pristine beach somewhere, some of these stories will open their eyes to the reality of life in rural Thailand.

Soon after I became a monk, I established a charity to support impoverished Thai students. The charity – the Students' Education Trust – provides scholarships to many hundreds of students at universities and at technical and vocational colleges. After I heard some of the novices' stories, a new SET scholarship programme was established specifically to help novice monks who felt that the religious life was not for them and who wanted to disrobe to study at vocational or technical colleges. Through the programme, many dozens of former novices have since gained technical qualifications. A few – including some of the novices featured in *Little Angels* – have even gone on to study at university for degrees. I am very happy to have been able to give them the opportunities they deserved.

1

Drop that mango!

I have lived as a Buddhist monk in Thailand for nearly ten years. I've lived in a monastery in Bangkok, one in a forest and one in a rural city. I've stayed briefly in many more during my travels around the country. They've all been very different monastic environments, but always the community has included at least a few novice monks, and sometimes dozens. The majority of novices are in their early to late teens but they can range in age from as young as seven, to as old as twenty. After twenty, a novice is usually expected to either ordain as a full monk or disrobe entirely. There are some exceptions. In a few monasteries, particularly in the international forest communities in the northeast of Thailand, novices may sometimes be much older than twenty. Within those communities, ordaining as a novice for a time may be seen as a way of testing a man's spiritual commitment to the monastic life, before he is allowed to become a monk.

Over the years I have observed, but generally ignored, hundreds of Thai novices. Those I have observed, even casually, have often been very different in background, intelligence, outlook, character and behaviour, as well as in age. Despite their obvious differences, like most of my Thai monk colleagues I always tended to lump them all together as simply 'novices'; naughty little orange-robed figures useful for running errands or doing odd jobs, but not much else, and of a different caste to the monks. It's not usually necessary for a monk even to know a novice's first name. The Thai word for novice, *nehn*, acts as a prefix to the boy's name and is normally sufficient in itself for addressing him.

Because I live within a country and culture that I do not entirely understand, and probably never will, I try not to be too judgemental about the people I come into contact with. I prefer to observe in a more neutral way if I can. But I do understand the Buddhist novice precepts and training rules. In recent years, I have had the experience, responsibility and pleasure of training many novices of my own. My novices have usually been young Westerners, but I also occasionally train Thai boys. Western or Thai, I know how novices are supposed to behave and the standards and ideals to which they, theoretically, should aspire. Based on that understanding and judged only within the framework of the precepts and training rules, I can safely say that a few of the novices I have observed have been excellent – 'little angels' indeed. The majority of them have been good, or at least reasonably well behaved, and some have been mediocre. A minority has definitely fallen into the 'little devils' category.

Before I ordained in Thailand, I think I must have been very naïve about the order of Buddhist monks. For nearly five years, as a layman, I had studied under and been trained by some excellent and very senior monks at Wat Buddhapadipa, the Thai monastery in London. I was forty when I started studying and some of my teachers had ordained as monks before I was even born. One, coincidentally, had become a monk on the very day I was born. There were no junior or new monks living in the monastery, and no novices.

In all my years of studying at the London monastery, and later when I lived there full-time in preparation for my own ordination, I never once saw even the slightest deliberate infringement of the monks' precepts by my teachers. By agreement amongst all the resident monks, some training rules had to be laid aside, or slightly bent, but that was a sensible and necessary compromise to time and place. The English weather isn't the same as that in India, where the precepts and rules were laid down, and it can be bitterly cold in winter. Some of the monks in London were quite old, which meant they sometimes needed to wrap up warmly in more than just the thin robes allowed by the rules. Thick socks, shoes, long johns, vests and assorted woolly undergarments (provided they couldn't be seen under the robes) were necessary and healthy precautions during the winter months. One lovely old monk used to venture out in winter wearing a woollen hat and scarf, an overcoat reaching down to his ankles and fur-lined snow boots. Besides sometimes compromising about clothes, the monks couldn't rely on getting food by walking on daily alms round, since they would have starved to death, so breakfast food was bought weekly at a supermarket. Common sense dictated that a few other rules had to be adapted too, though even that shocked some of the Thai lay-people who visited the monastery.

Despite the occasional necessary compromise, the monks never lost sight of the *spirit* of even the most minor rule. The example I received from those wise and dedicated teachers probably led me to expect unrealistically high standards of behaviour from all my brother monks, and even from the youngest novices, when I later ordained in Thailand.

After I ordained, the idealised view that I had earlier developed about monks' behaviour caused me occasional mental conflict. Sometimes, after seeing some particularly blatant breaking of the precepts or rules, it seemed to me that I was the only monk in Thailand who was putting in any effort at all. The Sangha simply didn't live up to my expectations. I desperately wanted it to but, of course, it couldn't. For a time, I became a real Sangha cynic. Happily, over the years I've become more realistic and I hope less pompous and self-righteous. I am now more concerned with my own practice than that of others and I now don't *expect* anything at all from anybody. By not expecting anything, by trying not to be judgemental, I am happy and even inspired when I see monks or novices practising well, but feel no disappointment when I see them practising badly, or not to some illusory and dreamy ideal standard of my own. Of course, there are many very excellent monks and novices in Thailand, but poor behaviour is generally more obvious than good and we usually only get to hear about the bad ones. Over the years, I've become convinced that the majority of Thai monks practise well, or at least as well as they can according to their own understanding of the teaching. That's all that any of us can do. I still retain a personal ideal standard for my own practice, but I now direct my criticisms and disappointments towards myself, when I also frequently don't live up to my own expectations.

One of the first incidents that helped shatter my

illusions about novices happened in my second year as a monk, when I moved to my present monastery in the north of Thailand. It was really a very minor incident, but at the time it seemed important, at least to me. My *kuti*, or monk's residence, is fairly isolated at the back of the monastery. At the time, the kuti was on the edge of a large area of wasteland that was covered with piles of rubbish, bushes and stunted trees. That's all concrete now. One evening, a few months after I moved to the monastery, I looked out from my kuti window and saw a little novice squatting down behind a bush, furtively eating a mango. Novices and monks are forbidden by their precepts from eating in the afternoon and evening and are supposed to fast between noon and the following dawn.

It seems silly now, but I was genuinely shocked to see a novice breaking one of his precepts. I shouted at him, 'Oi, you 'orrible little novice, drop that mango!' or something equally erudite. I'd shouted in English so he didn't understand me, but he dropped his forbidden fruit and scurried quickly away, terrified. The next time I saw him, I took him aside and quoted the relevant novice precept to him: 'I undertake the rule of training to refrain from eating at the wrong time.' I had to speak in Pali, since at that time my Pali was better than my Thai. He understood what I said, but just shrugged and laughed, apparently unconcerned and even surprised that I'd bothered to mention it. I regret that I made the instant and badly considered judgement that he was a 'bad' novice.

It wasn't long before I discovered that if I walked around the wasteland in the evening and poked at almost any bush, at least one little novice would jump out and run away laughing, his cheeks and pockets bulging with food of some kind or another. I did a lot of shouting in those early days but, after a while, the novices started avoiding the area around the kuti of the grumpy old foreign monk and went elsewhere for their evening picnics.

I realised that far from having just one badly behaved novice in the monastery, the majority of them were eating in the evening. They were openly misbehaving in other ways too, though I usually saw only quite minor infringements of the rules. I frequently saw novices, wearing only their wrap-around under-robes, playing football or climbing trees. The thin under-robe isn't the ideal garment to run about in, or for dangling from branches in, especially as novices don't have underwear. Not all novices are pre-pubescent little boys – some are well developed, strapping young men – and Thai monasteries are very public places. Besides being playgrounds for local children, there are often laywomen or even nuns wandering around the grounds. They could quite easily be offended, not just by accidental 'flashing', but by the fact of the misbehaviour itself. It probably seems very petty and there isn't a training rule that says 'thou shalt not climb trees', but the many rules about deportment are important and are intended to prevent undignified and immodest behaviour. The rules encourage constant mindfulness about bodily movements and should be followed, so that the monk or novice is always dignified, whatever he is doing.

I wondered why I seemed to be the only monk in the monastery who was bothered by this flagrant breaking of the novice precepts or training rules. Some very senior monks lived close to my kuti and they must have been aware of the novices eating food in the evening, climbing trees or playing football. They seemed unconcerned and never reprimanded them, though it is part of every monk's duty to do so if he sees a more junior monk or novice not practising properly. I occasionally even saw senior monks actually giving food to novices in the evening. Shocking!

It was only later, after I became more understanding and a bit more laid-back about such things, that I realised the senior monks' concern for sticking blindly to the rules was outweighed by their compassion for what were simply hungry little boys. Naughty novices, perhaps, but basically just ordinary little boys. I think I'd previously made too much of a distinction between 'little boy' and 'novice monk'. To me they were quite different beings and I expected them to behave in different ways. That realisation and understanding was a good lesson for me. It helped me to be much less rigid in my concepts of 'right' and 'wrong', 'good' and 'bad', especially where novices were concerned. I am happy to say (but may get criticised for saying it) that I now feel the same as some of the more compassionate senior monks and I also occasionally feed hungry little novices who, for whatever reason, missed their lunch. Or, indeed, who didn't miss lunch but are simply hungry.

A couple of years ago, I had my own group of six new Thai novices living within my kuti compound. They were the first Thai novices that I'd been given to train. I hadn't been looking forward to it much, thinking I'd have nothing but problems with them. The boys were all in their early teens and were the sons of high-ranking soldiers and policemen. The fathers felt their sons needed some spiritual discipline, so they had been ordered to ordain for a few weeks with the strict foreign monk as their teacher. I think the boys were dreading the experience as much as I was. They seemed quite terrified of me at first, but they were delightful lads and we got on very happily. Most of them were at private schools and all spoke English quite well. They tried hard to please me in their practice as novices, though I think mainly because they knew I was supposed to give a report to their fathers at the end of their time in the robes.

After a couple of days they all started to complain of being hungry in the evening. I explained that according to the rules they could only eat in the evening if they were sick and it was a medical necessity. I told them that I wouldn't compromise the rule. Overnight, an inexplicable plague descended on my small community. I had little boys rolling about on the floor, clutching their stomachs and groaning dramatically, and even drawing red and blue spots on their faces with felt tip pens. I eventually gave in and drew up a schedule that allowed them to take it in turns to eat a very small bowl of rice in the evening, one boy each evening, alone in a room, whilst his fellow novices salivated at the keyhole. So much for the strict foreign monk.

Not all precept or rule breaking is as minor or as frequent as climbing trees, playing football or eating in the evening. There are occasionally much more serious breaches of monastic discipline. In my monastery, a novice will sometimes be caught stealing from a donation box, or from the room of another novice or monk. (On one such occasion, the quick-thinking novice claimed he had his hand in the donation box so that he could dust the money.) It doesn't happen often, but theft cannot be condoned in any circumstances. If a novice really needs money for some genuine purpose, the abbot or a senior monk will always provide it. Such behaviour is always dealt with quickly and immediately: *get out now!* An older novice may be caught taking amphetamines (a major problem amongst Thai youth) and he must disrobe and leave the monastery the same day. I should stress that from my own observation, drug taking is rare in monasteries and, when such a case is discovered, the boy will usually have been addicted before ordaining. Few novices have the income to sustain such a habit anyway. Although major breaches of discipline are rare, they happen frequently enough that my abbot keeps a stock of second-hand shirts and trousers in his kuti which he will provide to the disrobing novice, so there is no delay in the disgraced boy's departure. Compassionately though, the Abbot will usually also provide a little money to the boy, at least enough for him to get back to his home town or village.

The most serious breach of discipline I ever saw happened very early one morning, before dawn. I got up at about 3.30am and was taking a stroll through the grounds. I saw a teenage boy, wearing a shirt, jeans and a baseball cap, climbing into the monastery over the back wall. He ran away when he saw me, but not before I recognised him as one of our older novices. I don't usually know what's going on in the monastery from day to day, so I assumed he must have disrobed as a novice. I thought nothing more about it but later that day, at the morning service, I saw him dressed in his robes again. I realised he was leading a sort of double life and going AWOL at night, perhaps to visit a girlfriend or for some other un-novice-like mischief. It's quite wrong for any monk to dismiss such behaviour as simply naughtiness, or to ignore it on compassionate grounds. That put me in a difficult position because really I had a duty to report the boy, but the abbot must have found out from somebody else because the novice was officially disrobed the next day.

Although I've seen plenty of examples of rule breaking, I have also observed a few quite exceptional novices whose behaviour, at least in public, has been perfect. Such novices have been diligent about walking on alms round every dawn, keeping total attention on their bowls, as they've been trained to do. They eat their food as though it was a meditation exercise, slowly and carefully, with 'mindfulness'. They attend the morning and evening service every day – something which few novices really enjoy – and have made an effort not only to learn, but also to understand, the difficult Pali chants. (Even after nearly ten years, I'm still hopeless at chanting.) Their robes are always worn neatly, they never run or seem to make any unconsidered movement, they speak only when necessary and then always politely and gently. They perform their duties willingly and without complaint and are always the first to volunteer when some job needs to be done. Sometimes, they may even be seen in quiet corners of the monastery, sitting in the full lotus position practising meditation, which is most unusual for a Thai novice. Everything about them says 'Buddhist novice monk'. I admire such novices greatly and very much hope that they enjoy the monastic life sufficiently to go on to ordain as monks when they are old enough.

Over the years, I've seen literally hundreds of novices come and go at my present monastery. Some have ordained only for a short time anyway, usually for a few weeks during the long school summer holiday when their parents don't know what else to do with them. Many monasteries organise a mass novice ordination during the holidays, with a month-long training programme for high school students. During their short stay, the new novices attend daily classes to learn about the life of the Buddha, his teaching, and perhaps some basic meditation. They are often enthusiastic to learn, but nobody expects them to become perfectly behaved novices in a month.

I have also observed longer-term novices, some of whom have spent more time in the robes than I have, but they tend to move around from monastery to monastery, perhaps as their novice friends move, or looking for a more conducive environment, a better school, and for many other reasons too. Some long-term novices that I have observed have stayed at my monastery for years, but I can't honestly say that I've become particularly friendly with any of them. We may exchange a friendly greeting when we pass, or what they think of as a friendly Western greeting: *'Hey you!'* or *'Oh my God, it's the Phra Farang!'* or something similar – but that's usually as far as it goes.

Senior or older monks don't usually become over-friendly with the much younger novices, though they are often very kind to them. A senior monk – one who has spent perhaps twenty years or more in the robes – would have to be at least forty years old, so there is always a great age difference between him and the novices. Senior monks tend to be fairly quiet and introspective anyway. They get on with their own practice, regardless of what anyone else is doing, and don't want to be bothered by the antics of the novices or younger monks in the community. They may never even know their names. The novices are usually quite wary of the senior monks, often have great respect for them and do not want to disturb them. I'm by no means a senior monk, but I am a foreign monk in my mid-fifties and therefore, status-wise in the monastery, a bit off to one side and difficult for anybody to pigeonhole. Consequently, the novices try not to bother me either and I don't have much contact with them or the young monks, or didn't have in my first few years at the monastery.

Although for the early years I had little or no contact with the novices, except to shout at them occasionally, I gradually become more acquainted with at least a few that I had seen around the monastery over a long period. Some of the less shy ones, or those less frightened of me, might ask me to teach them some simple English, try to get me to repeat some very rude Thai, or question me about English football teams – something I know absolutely nothing about. Sometimes we would get chatting. I soon discovered that although rarely 'little angels' as novices, they were delightful young people, almost without exception. I realised that even some of the older novices who, in my ignorance, I had mentally labelled as 'orange-robed yobs', were often very pleasant individuals. Outside of the context of their ability to keep the rules and precepts, none of them were bad lads by any means. Perhaps it was then, for the first time, I started to get a more realistic perspective of what exactly the Sangha was comprised of.

Whereas in London I had formed the silly and idealistic notion that everybody who wore the robes was dedicated to the teaching of the Buddha and aiming only towards 'perfection', I began to realise that the community in the monastery was made up of *real people*. Individuals: ordinary and extraordinary people, clever and stupid, ignorant and wise, arrogant and humble, sincere and insincere, young and old, but all with their own personalities, their good points and faults, their inner strengths and weaknesses, their personal successes and failures, and their own disappointments, frustrations, dreams and aspirations. I also realised that different people had different reasons for ordaining as monks or novices, and that those reasons sometimes had little to do with any genuine commitment to following the teaching of the Buddha.

As I got to know some of the novices a little better, I discovered that they all had their own very personal stories to tell. I enjoyed listening to their tales about life in their little rural villages – so different from my own far off and comfortable childhood in London – and their sometimes very moving tales of poverty and hardship, lack of opportunity, or the other circumstances that led to their ordaining as novices. I decided to try and record some of their stories, to understand their lives, and I became fascinated by what they had to say. *Little Angels* is the result.

2

Sorry son, you'll have to be a novice

The Western visitor to a Thai Buddhist monastery may sometimes be very surprised, perhaps even shocked, at the apparent casualness of life within its walls. Thai monasteries are largely autonomous and can vary greatly from each other, usually depending on the qualities, discipline and views of individual abbots. Generally speaking, the monasteries are quite different in atmosphere to those of other religious orders. Solemn, meditative monks gliding slowly and silently through ancient cloisters, kneeling in private prayer in tiny, bare cells, or joining others of the community in offering praise to God through inspired music or chants, bears little relationship to the hustle and bustle of the typical Thai Buddhist monastery.

Although not true of every Thai monastery, in some

the inspired music most likely to be heard is that of the latest pop singer, blaring out from the stereo of a young monk or novice. The silent night will often be shattered by the excited cheering of the monks and novices as they watch Manchester United or Arsenal on a late night TV sports programme, or a boxing match transmitted live from Europe. Poorly disciplined monks and novices, with little or no apparent concern for their training rules, may be seen wandering around public areas with their outer robes tossed casually over one shoulder, sometimes smoking cigarettes, laughing loudly and generally behaving as though they were at a resort, rather than in a monastery. On more than one occasion, I have even seen new monks smoking whilst walking on their morning alms round, or driving cars and motorcycles around monastery grounds.

At the other extreme, some Thai monasteries are very strict, though no more strict than they ought to be. Such monasteries tend to attract the best and most committed monks and novices; those who are determined to get as much as possible out of their time in the robes and who understand the importance of monastic discipline as a framework for their overall practice. These monasteries will usually be spotlessly clean and very quiet, with no TVs or radios to be heard at any time, no smoking allowed in public areas, and robes properly worn at all times. Walking on alms round every day, attending the morning and evening services, listening to Dhamma talks and sitting in meditation for long periods may be compulsory. Even some of the ancient precepts or training rules which may be considered out-of-date in many monasteries, or irrelevant to present-day Buddhism, will still be followed simply because they are rules. There are about 30,000 monasteries in Thailand, so between the two extremes there are many variations of disciplinary standards, but in every monastery the monks practise according to their individual understanding and their own sense of commitment, which may range from very great to non-existent.

Few Thai monasteries are closed to visitors and most are very public places. Some are in remote forest or mountain locations and are wonderfully peaceful, but most monasteries are in cities, towns and villages. They need to be because, traditionally, Buddhist monks and novices rely on the local lay community for all their daily needs, such as alms food and robes, and even for the materials to build their dwellings. In return for this material support, the monks give spiritual guidance and leadership to the lay community. The monks also preside at important cycle-of-life ceremonies, either in the monastery or in the home, so the monastic community generally develops hand-in-hand with the lay community, each reliant on the other.

Besides being the venue for religious festivals, merit-making ceremonies, Dhamma talks and funerals, Thai monasteries may also stage fund-raising fairs, public film shows and performances of traditional dance, music or drama. They are often the site of polling booths during local and national elections. In most rural communities, the government primary school may be located on the monastery's land, an arrangement which was the norm in Thailand until about seventy years ago, when the monks also acted as the school teachers.

Unlike the monasteries of some other religious orders, those in Thailand are not just the homes of reclusive monks and religious scholars, or of those who wish to spend their days in contemplation and meditation. Most monasteries in towns and cities provide free lodging for poor students studying at local schools or colleges and are often willing to take in boys who have problems at home. Depending on the outlook, compassion and sense of social responsibility of individual abbots, some monasteries may serve other important roles too. Besides, in the past, serving the early educational needs of local children, a few monasteries today may have significant social involvement, far beyond that which they routinely and traditionally have with the local community. Although the number of monasteries actively involved in social work is very small, there are those that combine monastery with orphanage, old people's home, youth reformatory or emergency public shelter. A few may act as refugee camps, AIDS hospices, abused women's shelters, drug addiction treatment centres and even animal shelters.

Some critics believe that the monks and monasteries shouldn't be socially involved at all, or not in such active and practical ways. Social or charitable work usually involves raising funds from the public, which to some traditionalists equates with 'business' and therefore falls outside the monks' role. To reformists, such an argument implies that it's acceptable to raise money to build yet another temple or Buddha image – something the Buddha never wanted – but unacceptable to raise funds to offer help to those who are suffering in some way, although compassion is a cornerstone of the Buddha's teaching. Traditionalists claim that the monasteries should act only as centres of religious learning, especially as the resident monks are not usually trained to cope with social problems. There may be some validity to their views, but the simple fact is that Thailand still has a long way to go in developing its welfare and social services. For the time being at least, some monasteries and monks give whatever help they can. Often they do it very well. Many already disadvantaged people would have no refuge at all without the monks' compassion and social involvement.

Besides being very public places and closely related

to the local community, monasteries in Thailand differ in a more fundamental way from those of some other religious orders. In other monastic communities, the monks and novices are usually there primarily because of their religious or spiritual convictions. Taking the vows of the order may be seen as a serious and life-long commitment. In Thailand, religious conviction is more likely to be at the bottom of the list of reasons for a man to ordain as a monk or a boy to become a novice.

In Thailand, short-term ordination as a monk is such an accepted tradition that government agencies and many large companies allow their male employees a one-time 'ordination leave', usually of three months. In popular Thai Buddhism, ordaining as a monk for a short period is seen as part of the rite-of-passage from youth to adulthood; part of becoming a 'complete' man. A man aged more than twenty, who has not yet ordained, is sometimes referred to in Thai as *dip* – unripe or immature. Most Thai men, soon after passing twenty, still follow tradition and ordain as monks for a time, usually during the three-months-long rainy season retreat, or *Pansa*. Despite ordaining mainly because of tradition, that's not to say that a Thai man who becomes a monk, even on a tempo-rary basis, doesn't have any religious convictions at all or, once ordained, will not try his best as a monk. Some don't bother but many others do, and there are some very fine monks in Thailand, even amongst the 'short-timers'.

'Making merit' is also an important aspect of popular Thai Buddhism and the best way to make merit is to ordain as a monk or novice. Many Thai people believe that the merit earned through even a short time spent in the robes can be passed on for the benefit of others, so ordaining is often a way of saying 'thank you' to parents, especially to mothers. Ordaining may also be a gesture showing remorse and to balance out some past mistake or bad behaviour. At funerals, it's common for even very young boys to ordain as novices just for the day of the funeral, to make merit on behalf of their deceased relative. I've seen such novices as young as four years old.

Many Thai men ordain for a longer period than the three months' rainy season retreat, perhaps immediately after finishing their higher education and before settling down to work and starting a family. They are often very committed to Buddhism and may remain as monks for two or three years, during which time they are able to study and understand the Buddha's teaching in much greater depth than the shorter term or temporary monks. After disrobing, they can apply that understanding in a practical way to their lives as laymen and family men. Sadly, a few of those who ordain for a longer period are simply lazy and can't be bothered to look for work, preferring to take advantage of the free accommodation, free food, and a small income from chanting blessings or taking part in funerals. For them, being a monk may be little more than a job.

Boys under twenty do not come under the same traditional cultural pressures to ordain as novices, except for the odd day or two when a member of the family dies. Whereas older men at least have some choice in whether to ordain as monks or not, young boys may often have no choice in the decision to become novices at all, which will more usually rest with their parents or guardians. The pressures on them are quite different from those faced by older men, but may be even stronger. For many boys, the pressure to ordain as novices stems entirely from family poverty and the lack of opportunity which inevitably follows.

Visitors to Thailand on the typical package tour itinerary – Bangkok, Chiang Mai, Phuket and so on – may be whisked from place to place by plane, coach or limousine. They will pass mainly through busy and prosperous-looking towns straddling main roads or motorways and may not fully appreciate that Thailand is really a nation of tiny, often remote, farming villages. The visitor may be forgiven for coming to the conclusion that almost everybody in Thailand is involved in the tourist, service or entertainment industry in some way. In fact, (according to the *Bangkok Post* newspaper in 2000) more than eighty per cent of the population is involved in farming of one sort or another. Most ordinary tourists never get to see the poorer, rural provinces of Thailand – in the northeastern region particularly – where the daily struggle with poverty, deprivation and hunger may be a basic fact of many lives.

In Thailand, few ordinary farmers become wealthy from their land. The majority remains desperately poor. In good years, years without drought, flood or pests, most farmers with small areas of owned or rented land are lucky if they can harvest enough rice, fruit and vegetables for their own family needs, with maybe a little left over to sell. Just finding sufficient money to feed the family and buy necessities can be a major difficulty for some. Many families become trapped in a spiralling cycle of poverty, debt and more poverty. In a survey conducted in 2000 amongst students at an agricultural college, the average estimated annual income of the students' farming parents was a little over 27,000 baht, which works out at just seventy-four baht a day, or about half the government's recommended minimum daily wage. Some claimed their parents earned as little as 10,000 baht a year from their backbreaking toil on the land. A hard life indeed, particularly for the children from such families.

One of my Thai teacher-monks at the London monastery once told me about his early childhood and the reason why he became a novice when he was about eight. He was born in a small, very poor village in the northeastern province of Srisaket. He told me that his rice-farming parents rented only a very small area of land and were almost destitute at times, sometimes to the point where they had no food to give him at all. During times of drought or flood, when crops could be lost entirely, the family simply starved. My teacher, as a little boy, would be forced to eat dirt. Eat dirt? I could hardly believe that, but some friends and I later stayed in the village and we watched a group of skinny little children eating the earth from a shallow ditch they had dug. (I later discovered that the type of earth they'd been eating contained nothing nutritious, but that something in it caused hunger pangs to temporarily subside.)

My teacher's parents became so desperately poor that they could no longer afford to keep their son at home, send him to primary school, or even feed or clothe him. They wanted to keep him at home, if only for the limited help he gave in the rice paddies, or in gathering edible plants and bugs from the forest. They eventually had no other option and common sense dictated that he would have to ordain as a novice at the village monastery, simply so that he would be assured of food each day. Because the monks and novices relied on the villagers for food, there wasn't always enough to eat in the monastery either, but it was better than nothing at all and certainly better than eating dirt.

On that same visit to my teacher's village, I met a stunted, bow-legged, seven-year-old boy named Gai. His mother had bled to death while giving birth to the boy after her mother had been forced to cut the baby from her daughter's womb with a machete, on the dirt floor of their shack. The father had already gone off with another woman, so Gai was brought up by his ancient grandmother in her tiny, wooden hut. The boy suffered from malnutrition, which wasn't surprising. Each day for the whole of his short life he had eaten only a handful of glutinous rice, mixed with the moths and bugs that his grandmother caught as they flew around a candle flame in the hut. He had never been to school. Like my teacher, Gai was ordained as a novice in the village's sleepy little monastery when he was about eight, simply so that he could be assured of food. Unlike my teacher, who soon moved to a monastery where he could study, Gai stayed in the village monastery until he was about fifteen, learning absolutely nothing. He eventually disrobed and went to look for manual work in Bangkok. As far as I know, he never returned to the village.

These two stories are not at all unusual in present-day rural Thailand, particularly in the northeast. Similar sad experiences could be related by hundreds of thousands of children from impoverished farming families. For the parents, having their sons ordained as novices in the local monastery is often the only answer to their problems. Maybe it sounds a bit heartless to a Westerner, who might immediately think in terms of the boy's lost childhood, but it's not usually a case of the parents simply dumping their responsibilities on to the monastery. It may be the only practical solution to ensure any future at all for the child.

Even if a family is able to feed its children properly, a desperate shortage of money may mean that anything beyond that is a luxury, including even basic education. Six years of primary education and three years at high school is currently compulsory and free at government schools in Thailand, but fees must usually be paid from fourth to sixth grade of high school. The diploma for completing sixth grade is almost the minimum requirement for getting any sort of decent job at all. The government plans to extend the free and compulsory education to twelve years, but to many impoverished families that won't make any difference. Despite the early free tuition, many children are unable to study at high school and some do not even complete their primary education. Even at eight or nine years old, children may be needed to labour in the rice paddies or to contribute towards the family income in some other way. Often, children cannot go to school simply because the parents can't afford to pay for the required uniform and shoes, or books, pencils, bus fares, daily lunch and all the other expenses associated with education. In Thailand, a country that sometimes seems almost obsessed with uniforms, if you don't have the right clothes, you can't have the education. I knew two teenage girls who lived near to my monastery and who attended a local vocational college. Their parents could only afford to buy one uniform, so the girls took it in turns to go to college on alternate days.

The only way for many parents to ensure even the most basic secular education for a son is to have the boy ordained as a novice, since he can then take advantage of the free tuition offered by some monasteries. That may sometimes be primary education, or high school, or both. The standard of education at the schools is sometimes very poor, but there are no fees, accommodation costs, food costs, uniform costs or any other expenses for the parents to find. The arrangement may not always suit the boys themselves, but they have little or no choice in the matter. Thai children tend to be very obedient and will usually follow their parents' wishes without argument, stoically trying to make the best of any situation. Although the boy may not like the idea of becoming a novice – a very restrictive life for an active adolescent – or of living away from home, many may be desperate enough for an education that they go along with the idea. For some, the possibility of any future other than following in their parents' weary footsteps and becoming rice farmers would be welcome.

Unfortunately for the boy as well as the family, there are few good monastic schools teaching a secular curriculum in remote rural areas; the better ones are usually in towns and cities. Attending even an average monastic high school may mean moving a very long distance from home, perhaps even to another province. Once there, a lack of funds or pocket money from home may mean that the novice is only rarely able to visit his family. Sometimes, years may pass before he is able to return to his village again.

There are 4,000 monastic schools in Thailand. They vary greatly, not just in their standards, but also in their curricula. Because monasteries are largely autonomous, their standards and curricula depend to a great extent on the outlook of individual abbots, while their facilities depend on the generosity of the local community. Some monastic schools offer tuition only in religious subjects with monks as the teachers. Others offer a normal secular primary or high school education (but always with religious instruction too) and rely on volunteers or paid professional lay teachers, as well as monks.

I live in Nakhon Sawan, a city in the north of Thailand. In the city, we have two important monasteries, one vast and one tiny, and each with its own very different school. Both of the abbots are, in my opinion, very fine monks and both have high ecclesiastical rank, but they differ greatly in outlook. At the larger monastery, the abbot is a traditionalist. He believes that his novices only need to learn Dhamma and the Pali language, to prepare them to become monks, which he seems to imagine they all want to do. In his view, Science, Mathematics, English, Thai, Art or History need play no part in the school curriculum and are unnecessary subjects for novices to learn. The abbot allows his novices to attend a non-formal government school outside the monastery, but only for one day each week and providing it doesn't interfere with their religious studies or monastic duties. (Non-Formal schools are for students of any age who, for whatever reason, missed their primary or high school education.) The monastery has a magnificent school, capable of seating about a thousand novice and monk students. It rarely has more than twenty, except in the rainy season when the temporary monks ordain; then it increases to about fifty. All the students are resident at the monastery.

The other monastery is very small and cramped and located in a noisy and busy part of the city. It covers about one-tenth the area of the larger monastery but is home to four times as many monks and novices. The abbot, although a very senior and high-ranking monk, as well as a Pali scholar, is still a relatively young man.

He has a less traditional outlook than some other abbots. He seems to understand that few novices genuinely want to go on to become monks or spend the rest of their lives in the robes, so he realistically tries to prepare them for life after they disrobe. His monastery's school is capable of accommodating only about 200 students, but it teaches a full secular curriculum and it's packed with novices and young monks who travel daily from monasteries from miles around.

Between these two extremes there are many hundreds of other monastic schools too; traditional or progressive, small, medium or large, well equipped or with no facilities at all. Some have high standards and dedicated teachers, others have not. A new novice, determined to learn, may move around from one monastic school to another, looking for the one that he thinks is able to provide the education he needs, or which can further his progress in some way. To another new novice from a poor rural family, perhaps the opportunity to gain any education at all is better than nothing.

Most novices live in the monastery at which they study. Their accommodation can vary considerably, particularly between rural and city areas. One within a poor rural community may have only the most basic facilities, reflecting the poverty of the village. There, the novices may all be crammed into an old, falling down, wooden kuti, share a tiny room with others in a poorly built breeze-block building, or each may have little more than a plastic mat in an odd corner somewhere. That may still be better than the conditions they were used to at home.

Those who live in grander and wealthier city monasteries are likely to have much better accommodation. At my monastery, the most important in the province, each novice and monk has his own reasonable-sized room in a large, modern kuti block. At the small monastery with the popular school, the rooms for novices are about the same size as those in my monastery, but each has as many as six novices packed into the space. The novices who live there are prepared to put up with the cramped quarters and endure the discomfort and inconvenience in return for their good-quality education.

Most monastic schools are closed on the weekly *Wan Phra*, or 'monk day', but that doesn't mean the novices get a day off. Besides usually studying five or six days each week, novices in town or city monasteries often have a very busy schedule outside the classroom as well. Before going to school, all novices should walk on the dawn alms round and they should attend the morning and evening services with the monks, when they chant passages from the Buddha's teachings. The chants – there are hundreds of them and some are very long – are in Pali, but the novices are expected to know their meaning and to learn at least the most commonly used ones by heart.

Each novice may have his own particular duties or responsibilities too, such as ringing the bell for morning and evening services, emptying rubbish bins, keeping the monastery grounds swept clean, cutting grass, preparing candles and incense for ceremonies, running errands for the monks or doing any other odd jobs that need to be done. In monasteries with crematoria, if the novices know the relevant chanting they may also join with the monks at funerals. Relatives of the deceased will usually make a small gift of money to the monks and novices who chant, which may be the only source of income for many novices. In my monastery, the gift may vary from 20 baht to 100 baht. Sometimes, a novice may be the personal attendant of a senior monk or teacher. In that case, his duties will be to help and serve the monk in any way that is needed, such as keeping his room swept and tidy, washing his alms bowl, robes and so on. In return, the monk will train and take care of the novice and may sometimes reward him with small amounts of money if the novice has some particular need. It can be a busy life for the novice. Even if he gets up at about 5am to walk on alms round and goes to bed at about 11pm, he may only have an hour or so in between as free time.

Novices who stay in small, rural monasteries without

schools may have less to occupy their time; sometimes nothing at all apart from a few simple cleaning duties. Perhaps that suits them. Novices who are prepared to move far away from their families, home village and the local monastery are usually those who are most motivated to find an education, while those who stay behind may be less so.

Although novices in busy city monasteries often have little free time, there's not usually much in the way of entertainment for them anyway. They are discouraged from leaving the monastery, since there is usually no need for them to do so unless they have some specific errand. Within the monastery, there may be a television somewhere, but any free time is usually spent studying, doing homework, sleeping, or chatting with their novice friends. Abbots generally like to keep the novices under their care as busy as possible, perhaps working on the principle that 'the devil makes work for idle hands'.

3

Rules, rules and more rules

Whichever way he turns, the novice is confronted by a precept or training rule, though he has considerably fewer precepts than a monk. The novice has only ten precepts but he must also follow seventy-five rules that are included in the monks' training, as well as many other traditional rules. The precepts and training rules govern every aspect of the novice's daily activities and behaviour, from how he should wear his robes, how he should walk, sit and eat, when and to whom he may teach Dhamma (not to someone wearing a hat, for example) and even how and where he may urinate, defecate or spit.

There's no getting round the precepts or training rules, despite the most ingenious and earnest efforts by some novices to try. None of the precepts or rules is open to convenient personal interpretation and all are very precisely defined in the Buddhist commentaries by a list of conditioning factors. Since the novice precepts and rules apply to young men and adolescent boys (as well as to monks, of course), even 'intentional emission of semen' is thoughtfully defined to such an extent that there's just no way to do it without breaking the rule (which is, of course, *don't*).

Despite the very precise definitions and qualifications, there will always be some novices who try to find a way around the precepts and rules, and probably have been for the past 2,500 years. One little novice I spoke with admitted that he regularly broke the precept of not eating in the evening but he claimed he followed the Buddhist 'Middle Way' – eating neither too much, nor too little. Another told me he would never eat rice in the evening, because the Buddha didn't, but it was therefore okay to eat cake. If that's the case, bring on the pizza.

The novices' ten precepts are: *I undertake the rule of training to refrain from:* taking life, taking what is not given, being unchaste, speaking falsely, taking distilled and fermented intoxicants or drugs, taking food at the wrong time, dancing, singing, playing music and seeing shows, using flowers, perfumes and cosmetics for beautifying and adorning the body, using high and luxurious sleeping places and seats, accepting gold and silver (money).

According to Buddhist histories, the precepts were laid down by the Buddha after his seven-year-old son, Rahula, became the very first novice monk. As more young men and boys became novices, so the Buddha then laid down various penalties for misbehaviour. After Rahula became a novice, the Buddha's father was distressed that he had lost first his son and then his grandson to the mendicant way of life when he had hoped they would follow in his footsteps and become rulers. He asked the Buddha to allow boys to ordain as novices only if they had their parents' permission, since otherwise the parents could suffer grief for the loss of their sons. The Buddha agreed and made it an offence for any monk to ordain a boy as a novice without parental permission. The rule still stands today.

Before a boy becomes a novice, he must first assure the senior monk who is to ordain him that he has his parents' permission, though usually the parents will be present anyway. The boy's head and eyebrows are then shaved before he requests the ten novice precepts from the monk. Requesting and repeating the ten precepts makes the boy into a novice and the seventy-five training rules are an additional support and a guide to help him regulate his behaviour and live his life as a novice in a blameless way. The novice ordination is usually a short and simple ceremony lasting about ten minutes. During the ceremony, the boy changes from his ordinary clothes into the robes of a novice. After the ceremony, the new novice usually makes a small gift to the monk, and the parents pay their respects by bowing not only to the monk but also to their son, the new novice, since he has been elevated to a higher social position than their own.

The novice's robes are exactly the same as those of the monk; an under-robe or waist-cloth (*sabong*) held up by a cord belt, a thin 'waistcoat' (*ungsa*) which covers his chest, and the outer robe (*jivorn*). The novice does not wear the additional robe (*sanghati*), which is folded into a long rectangle and draped over the monk's left shoulder during monastic ceremonies.

Like the five precepts of Buddhist lay people, or the 227 of the monks, the ten novice precepts should not be understood or practised at face value only. For example, the precept 'to refrain from taking what is not given' would obviously seem to refer to stealing, but if given thought and as a broader training for a moral and ethical life, it can mean more than that. 'Taking what is not given' can include even borrowing or moving something without the owner's permission, in case it inconveniences the owner, so the precept helps the novice develop a responsible attitude towards the property of others. Similarly with the other novice precepts. They must be understood in their full depth and meaning, rather than just practised superficially.

A few of the precepts may seem irrelevant to modern times, such as not sleeping on a high bed. Others may sound antiquated, such as not adorning oneself with flowers. The wording obviously reflects the social and cultural norms of the time when the Buddha laid down the precepts in India many centuries ago. But if the spirit as well as the wording of the precepts is taken into account, they remain just as valid now as they were originally. High beds and seats were probably considered luxurious in the Buddha's time. Modern novices may not wish to decorate themselves with flower garlands but, conditioned as they are by television commercials and other media, they may still be tempted to use perfumed deodorants, face creams and other cosmetics which they think make them more attractive. That's considered unnecessary and undesirable for those who are, theoretically at least, living the monastic or religious life. Novices and monks should live their lives without unnecessary luxury, comfort or sensual diversion, and keep their material needs as few and as basic as possible.

At most monasteries, the novices chant their precepts in Pali at the morning or evening services, or both. Once every two weeks, they renew their vows entirely (since they're bound to have broken one precept or another), thus becoming new and 'pure' novices again. At many monasteries, the novices also join with the monks in chanting the training rules every morning.

The novice's seventy-five training rules include: keeping his body properly covered with neatly wrapped robes, not to laugh loudly in inhabited areas, not to fidget any part of his body when sitting or walking and to keep his eyes downcast a plough's length ahead. Concerning food, the novice must accept alms food from lay-people mindfully, eat anything which is in the bowl without preference, eat with small mouthfuls, not speak when eating, not make slurping or chewing noises and not lick his fingers or lips. The novice cannot teach Dhamma to people sitting higher than him, walking in front of him, or holding umbrellas, sticks, knives or other weapons, wearing shoes, or sitting in a vehicle or easy chair. He should not urinate standing up, nor on to green vegetation or into streams or ponds, nor should he spit into them.

Besides his ten precepts and seventy-five training rules, the novice must follow other rules too. Some offences against the rules carry the penalty of expulsion, which in some monasteries may mean disrobing, rather than just being sent away. Breaking other precepts or rules results in a heavy penalty without expulsion, and for some a lighter penalty decided and imposed by the novice's teacher or a senior monk. According to a commentary about the training of novices, written by a former Supreme Patriarch of the Thai Sangha, the precepts and rules which carry penalties can be grouped and described briefly as follows:

The ten expulsion offences

1. Taking life.
2. Taking what is not given.
3. Being unchaste.
4. Speaking falsely.
5. Taking intoxicants.
6. Defaming the Buddha.
7. Defaming the Dhamma.
8. Defaming the Sangha.
9. Holding wrong views.
10. Seducing Buddhist nuns.

The five heavy penalty offences for gross misconduct

1. Intentional emission of semen (except in a dream).
2. Lustfully engaging in bodily contact with a woman.
3. Addressing a woman with lewd words.
4. Attempting to persuade a woman to have sexual intercourse.
5. Acting as a go-between for a man and woman

for any matter concerned with their personal relationship.

The ten light penalty offences

1. Eating at the wrong time.
2. Taking part in or attending dancing, singing, playing music or watching shows.
3. Using flowers, perfumes and cosmetics to beautify and adorn the body.
4. Using luxurious couches, beds or seats.
5. Accepting gold or silver (ie, money).
6. Seeking to deprive monks of their gains.
7. Seeking what is not beneficial for monks.
8. Seeking to make a monk leave his place of residence.
9. Insulting monks.
10. Causing disharmony between monks.

If all the precepts and other rules were not enough, there are also many hundreds of Thai monastic and cultural traditions that the novice has to remember, though some do not stem from Buddhism at all. The novice should duck or lower his head as he passes in front of a monk or Buddha image and not point his feet at a monk or Buddha image. He should hold his hands in the prayer-like position when speaking to a monk, never sit higher than a monk and use both hands to pass something to a monk. There are many, many more. They don't carry penalties, but if the novice forgets them he is likely to be considered impolite and may be reprimanded by the monks.

Although a minority of novices may appear not to care about their precepts and training rules at all, every novice should take them seriously, even if they can only manage to do so when under public scrutiny. Most do. Lay people are often as aware of the precepts and rules as the novices themselves; sometimes more so. A strict Buddhist lay-person may complain to the abbot if one of his monks or novices is seen to be behaving badly or breaking a precept and is completely justified in complaining. Monks and novices are supposed to set an example to the lay-people by practising well, so helping the people to sustain their faith in the Triple Gem: Buddha, Dhamma and Sangha. In return, the lay-people support the monks and novices for their material needs. If the monks and novices don't behave according to their precepts and training rules, they will not receive the support or respect they need and the Sangha cannot survive.

At my own monastery, there's sometimes a 'mass whacking' of novices by the abbot. It doesn't happen often, no more than a couple of times a year, and then usually only after a lay-person has made a complaint to the abbot about the novices playing football, or some similar minor breach in which they've all been involved. Because a lay-person has complained, and if after investigation the complaint is considered justified, some light punishment has to be seen to be given. The abbot calls all the novices together in the main temple hall, with the monks as witnesses, and instructs a monk to cut a few thin canes from a tree. After a lecture about correct behaviour, the novices line up for several strokes each on their backsides. They try hard to stifle their giggles and to look suitably admonished, but our dear abbot is quite old and fat and can't really get any strength behind his swings. I don't think his heart is in it anyway and I doubt if it really hurts the novices at all. The novices are wearing their outer robes and will usually have been warned in advance by a friendly monk, so they wear several layers of under-robes as well to help cushion the blows. It does help remind them, though, that the rules are important and should be kept.

Because of some widely publicised cases of extreme bad behaviour by a few monks, the entire Thai Sangha is presently under very close media and public scrutiny. That makes the novice, as well as the monk, very vulnerable and he must do his best to make his behaviour beyond reproach at all times. Sadly, false and malicious accusations by lay-people of serious breaches of monastic discipline are not unknown either, when the accuser bears a grudge for some reason.

At my monastery, an angry mother complained to the abbot that her fourteen-year-old daughter had been sexually molested by one of our older novices. He was about nineteen. The novice was known to be very well behaved and although the abbot doubted that the accusation was true, he was obliged to summon the boy and interview him, with the mother and daughter present. The novice vehemently denied the charge, but the abbot felt that a doubt remained and that he couldn't take a chance or put the monastery's reputation at risk. He told the novice he would have to disrobe. That would have been a disaster for the boy. He had been a novice for about ten years and was almost old enough to ordain as a monk, which he very much wanted to do.

In a way it was lucky that the foolish girl then additionally accused two of our most senior monks of molesting her as well. That was obviously nonsense, but her accusation against the monks made the whole issue a lot more serious and took it out of the abbot's hands. The police were called and the two monks and the novice spent eight hours at the police station being interrogated, photographed and fingerprinted. The wretched girl eventually admitted she had made the stories up because she was in love with the novice and was angry that he showed no interest in her. Unfortunately, the arrest of the three came at the time of a media witch hunt of bad monks and was reported in the Thai popular newspapers, with pictures, causing very great embarrassment to the three, to the abbot, and to our monastic community as a whole. Sadly, the later story of their innocence was not reported.

4

Novice Bom

*'Sometimes it's difficult being a 15-year-old
novice'*

When I was a little boy in my village, I had a lot of respect for the monks and novices at our local monastery. I thought even the youngest novices were very strict about keeping their precepts. I saw them walking on alms round each morning and they seemed so well behaved and disciplined. I never saw them break their rules and they inspired me to want to be a good boy. As a novice myself, I've since lived in several monasteries. I know now that the behaviour of the monks and novices when they are in private is not always good. Some just put on an act when lay-people are around.

When I read about bad monks or novices in the newspapers, I get worried that people might think all monks and novices are the same. They're not. I admit I'm not always so well behaved myself – sometimes I'm very naughty – but many novices really try to follow their precepts and rules and practise well. They try hard to be a model of good behaviour for the lay-people. Others don't care, but that's the same whether people are monks, novices or lay-people, rich or poor; there are always some good and some bad. Even Thai politicians don't always follow the five precepts or the teaching of the Buddha, even though they should also set an example to the ordinary people. I'm only a little novice of fifteen, so the only way I can help people is by doing my best to behave properly and follow the precepts. But sometimes it's difficult and I don't make a very good job of it.

I think the precepts are very important, whether for monks, novices or lay-people. The precepts are easy to understand, but they can be hard to keep. We can't just chant them everyday in the temple hall, read about them in books or remember them in our minds. That's easy, but we have to practise them in our daily life too, even if the best we can do is only to know when we've broken a precept and made a mistake. Then at least we can try to do better in future.

Everybody has the same first precept, about not taking life. That one's especially difficult. Even when we just walk about, we may accidentally tread on tiny insects and kill them. But if we don't mean to kill them, I think that makes a difference. I know the insect would still be dead, but the difference would be in our own minds and we would have done an accidentally bad thing, rather than a deliberately bad thing. I'd never kill anything deliberately, not even a mosquito or ant, even if they bit me. Well, maybe I would if they bit me because that's the habit I got into before I understood the precepts, but I have to try and gradually change my behaviour. I expect when the Buddha walked about in the forest he must have trodden on little insects, but I'm sure he never meant to because he was so kind. I think the Buddha was the kindest man who ever lived.

I think the fourth precept can be difficult too, about always telling the truth. Sometimes you have to tell a lie to protect yourself. For example, if I see a big novice doing something bad, he might threaten to beat me up if I tell anybody. If the abbot asked me if I saw the novice doing that thing, I'd have to say I didn't, so that would be a lie, but at least I wouldn't get beaten up.

I think the sixth precept, about not eating after midday, isn't helpful for a novice. I'm a young boy and if I don't eat in the evening I get a stomach ache, so I think it's sensible to eat. Novices and monks aren't supposed to eat a lot in case it makes us too sleepy for meditation, but I've never been taught meditation and

I don't think it would be very interesting anyway. One time, my abbot caught me eating in the evening and he scolded me. He told me I was a very bad novice and made me do a lot of extra sweeping as a punishment. After I used up all my energy sweeping, I was hungry again and had to eat some more. I was sorry about breaking the precept, but maybe the abbot doesn't get as hungry as me. I don't understand how he can eat so little, but still be so fat.

When I break the third novice precept about . . . you know . . . I'm always ashamed of myself because it means I don't have respect for the Lord Buddha or the precepts he gave to us novices. I do really, but it's very difficult to be a fifteen-year-old novice sometimes.

I've been a novice for three years, since I was twelve. My village is in the northeastern region of Thailand, in a province called Burirum. Thai people call the region Esarn. It's very dry and dusty and some areas can hardly support life at all. There used to be lots of forests in the region but they've mostly gone now. Esarn is very different from the rest of Thailand. We have our own culture, dress, food, music and language. We even look a bit different to Thais from other regions because our skins are sometimes darker and our noses are often broader and flatter. Most people who live in Esarn are descended from Laotian people and everybody in my village speaks Laos. When I go home for a visit, I have to change my language from Thai to Laos because some old people in the village can hardly speak Thai at all. Our food is spicier than food in other parts of Thailand. Many people think that some of the things we eat are horrible, like fried grasshoppers, caterpillars and ants' eggs – just about anything, really – but I like Esarn food very much. In Laos we say *sap ilie*; very delicious. We don't usually have many tourists in Esarn, except for a few backpackers, because we're not near the sea and don't have many smart resorts, but there are lots of interesting things to see and do. We have some beautiful ruins from the time when the region was part of the Cambodian Empire.

Some people from other parts of Thailand look down on Esarn people. They think we're not as cultured as they are and that we're uneducated and poor. It's true, most Esarn people are poor and many are uneducated, but that's not their fault. It doesn't mean we're all stupid. It's difficult to make a living on the land in the northeast, so many young Esarn people move to the cities where they usually get work as labourers, building new office blocks, apartments and hotels for rich people. They don't earn much money and they have to live in shantytowns or slums, or even under bridges. Esarn people usually care about their families a lot, so they try to send money home every month to their parents in the village. Esarn people work hard and sometimes have a difficult and unhappy life, but they don't complain much. Even though they have a hard life, I think Esarn people are a lot friendlier and happier in their hearts than people from some other parts of Thailand.

My village has about seventy-five houses and about 150 people, and it's far from anywhere. All the people are rice farmers, but rice farming is difficult in that area because the soil isn't very good and sometimes there isn't enough water. In some parts of Thailand, farmers can get two or more crops of rice each year, but in Esarn we usually only get one. My parents rent their land, but they only have about one acre. If there's enough water, they can earn about 8,000 baht a year from the rice crop. That's not much, considering there were seven people in my family when I lived at home. Some years, when there was drought, the village had no rice crop at all and then all the families were very poor.

I don't remember anything about my mother because my parents separated when I was a year old. I never saw my mother again after that. When I was a little older, I used to get upset when the other village children made fun of me, because I was the only boy without a mother. They told me my mother ran away because she didn't like me and because I was such an ugly baby. I didn't think that was true, but sometimes I cried about it. My father was very kind to me and I loved him, but I wanted a mother too so I could be as happy as my friends. My father remarried when I was about five years old. Sometimes, in stories, the step-mother is horrible to her new children but I was lucky because my stepmother became just like a real mother to me. She loved me and cared for me as though I was her own son, so I was happy then. I love her and miss her a lot, but the monastery I live at now is very far from my village and the journey takes about thirteen hours on the bus. I haven't been able to go home for a long time because the bus is too expensive.

The last time I saw my parents was about two years ago on *Songkran*, or Thai New Year's Day. That's the festival when we throw water over each other. Thai families always try to get back together at that time. I didn't have enough money to get home and I was very sad, but then a kind old monk gave me the bus fare. The journey was very tiring but I was excited about seeing my family again. All my brothers and sisters working in Bangkok went home for the festival and I think it was the happiest day of my life. We all laughed and cried a lot because we were so glad to be reunited.

Before that, the happiest day of my life was when I was ten years old and bought a pair of trainer shoes. I wanted them so much because I thought they would make me look like a modern city boy instead of a poor village boy. For eight months, instead of buying lunch at school with the money my father gave me each day, I secretly saved it until I had 400 baht, then I bought the trainers. I was so proud the first time I wore them. My friends were very jealous of me because they only had old sandals or nothing at all. But the trainers fell apart after about a week and then my friends laughed at me. They told me how foolish I'd been to waste my father's money, just to look good. I cried about the trainers, but I also cried about my own stupidity and selfishness. I realised that the things we can buy with money can't really make us as happy as more important things, like our love for our family or the respect of our friends. That was a good lesson to learn from a pair of trainers.

After my father remarried, I was always happy. I had lots of friends in the village and we enjoyed fishing or hunting for lizards and birds with our catapults. Thai people are very accurate with their catapults and they can be very dangerous weapons, especially if you are a lizard or bird. We never had enough time for playing though, because we all had many duties in the fields or around the house. My duty was to get up very early to cook the rice for breakfast. Esarn people eat 'sticky rice', which isn't the same as the rice most Thai people eat. We eat it with fermented fish sauce called *plah*, which some people say smells very bad, but I think it's delicious. Although sometimes we didn't have very much rice, I always cooked a little more than the family needed, so I could give some to the monks and novices from the village monastery when they walked by on their alms round. That was a good thing to do, because the Buddha taught us that we should be generous and share what we have with other people, even if we're poor. I agree with that.

After I finished my primary education at the village school, I didn't know what to do next. My parents couldn't afford the bus fares to send me to high school, so I thought I would either have to work in the paddy fields or maybe go to Bangkok or Pattaya to look for a job. I didn't really want to do either. Rice farming is very hard work but I'd heard bad things about the cities and what could happen to a young boy. I was only twelve and didn't have much idea about the future, but I really wanted to study for my high school certificate. My parents didn't have enough money for that, so I had to work in the fields. It wasn't too bad because a lot of my friends worked in nearby fields, so we were able to play as much as work.

One day, my father discovered that I'd taken an amphetamine pill. My friend gave it to me while we were working in the fields. He gave me a whole pill but I broke it in half and threw the other half away when he wasn't looking. I hope a chicken didn't eat it. I didn't really want to take even half the pill but the other boys took them and I didn't want to be the odd one out. I'd never taken any drugs before and I didn't like the effect it had on me. I knew I'd been stupid. It's probably a good thing that someone told my father, because he had a long talk with me that night. He wasn't angry with me, but I think he realised that he had to get me away from the other village boys.

My father suggested that I should become a novice. Besides wanting to stop me getting involved with drugs, I knew my parents had a problem about looking after all their children, even though they loved us very much. If I ordained as a novice, I wouldn't be a financial burden on them any more because I would be living in a monastery. I had mixed feelings about being a novice but I kept them to myself because I didn't want to disappoint my father, or make his life more difficult. I thought being a novice would be too hard for me, because I was quite naughty sometimes. I still thought then that all monks and novices kept their precepts strictly and I knew I probably wouldn't be able to. I was frightened that if I broke a precept, something bad would happen to me in the future. My father was a novice for two years when he was a little boy and he explained many things about the monastic life to me, so then I wasn't as nervous. But I was right about something bad happening to me if I broke a precept, because I had a terrible fright a few weeks after I ordained.

I became a novice in our village monastery when I was twelve. There were seven old monks in the monastery and some of them had been there for ever. There were also six novices of about the same age as me. I knew all the boys already, so I had some friends in the monastery and wasn't lonely. I also saw my parents every morning when I walked past our house on alms round. It was funny that when I saw my parents they paid respect to me, rather than the other way round. I was a bit embarrassed at first, but that's Thai tradition when a son is a monk or novice. The monastery was very quiet and none of us had much to do except sweep the grounds. I couldn't study there and I became quite lazy, just sleeping most of the time like the rest of the monks and novices. It was lucky really that I later had such a fright, otherwise I might have just stayed there for the rest of my life. One evening, I broke a precept by eating rice, and that same night a horrible ghost came after me.

I'd always been frightened of ghosts, but I'd never seen one before. The other novices had told me there was a ghost living in a big old tree in the monastery grounds. I wasn't sure whether to believe them but I was only a little boy and their stories scared me. I told the abbot I was scared, so he tattooed my arms and chest with four small pictures of magical birds and fish and he told me they would keep the ghost away. The needle hurt and the tattoos didn't work anyway.

One evening, I was very hungry and I ate some rice secretly in my room. That was the first time I did that and I felt ashamed afterwards about breaking my precept. Later, I had to walk through the grounds to go to the bathroom. It was very dark and I was just walking past the old tree when I suddenly felt sure someone or something was watching me. I was nearly stiff with fright, but I turned around very slowly. There was the ghost, standing behind the tree, staring at me with huge, round eyes. He was about twenty feet tall and had a very skinny body, except for his belly, which was fat and round. He had long thin legs and arms that hung down to his knees. His hands had very long fingernails and his white hair was dirty and tangled, hanging over his shoulders and down his back. He didn't have any clothes on at all, not even a piece of rag to cover his *bughum*. He had a tiny mouth in the middle of a very ugly face. I knew what it was – it was a *Peta* ghost!

I don't know if Peta ghosts live in other countries too, but we have a lot of them in Thailand. They are very greedy but can never be satisfied, because their bellies are big but their mouths are tiny, so they have to keep eating all the time. Some Thai people believe that if you are a very greedy person, always wanting more and more of everything, you will be reborn as a Peta. I knew the Peta had come for me because I'd eaten rice in the evening. For a moment I couldn't move, but then I screamed and ran back to the kuti, not looking behind me because I was sure he was chasing me, to punish me for being a bad and greedy novice.

I ran to the abbot's kuti and banged on the door. He let me in and asked me what was wrong, but at first I was too frightened to talk and just sobbed. After he calmed me down, I told him what I'd seen. I confessed that I'd broken a precept and eaten some rice. The abbot hung a small Buddha amulet around my neck and said that it would protect me. He said the Peta wouldn't come after me any more because I regretted eating in the evening and had promised not to do it again.

After that terrible experience I decided I would leave the monastery and move to another one far away, and then get on with my high school studies. I also promised myself to try a bit harder at keeping the precepts, because I didn't want any more ghosts coming after me. I knew a novice who lived in a monastery in Nakhon Sawan Province and he said it had a good school and no ghosts. It was more than two hundred kilometres away from my village, which was far enough, I thought. My parents were very sad that I was leaving the village. They knew they wouldn't see me for a long time but they understood that I wanted to get an education. I was sad too, but I tried hard to act like a proper novice and not cry when I said goodbye to my mother. I cried later, on the bus.

The monastery in Nakhon Sawan was in the centre of the noisy city. I didn't like it much. Although I was trying harder to be a good novice and keep my precepts, the abbot was too strict and often scolded the novices for no reason. It seemed to us that if we were going to be scolded for something we hadn't done, we might just as well do it anyway, so sometimes we did. I wasn't happy living there and I became quite miserable. After several months, some of the novices decided to move to another monastery close by, so that's how I came to live at Wat Worranatbanpot. We usually call the monastery 'Wat Kob', which means Frog Temple. There, I have a nice big room and plenty of food from alms round. My room has mosquito screens, an electric fan and a wooden parquet floor, which I'd never seen before. It seems very luxurious to me, compared to my family home. Because the monastery is so big, there are lots of areas where the novices can secretly play, out of the abbot's sight. I'm much happier at that monastery, but the abbot there is also very strict with the novices, especially if he sees us playing football. If he catches us, we all get a few strokes of the cane, but he doesn't catch us very often, thank goodness.

Although it's against the novices' rules about behaviour, I think we should be allowed to play football because it's good exercise for young boys. Apart from walking on alms round every morning and sweeping around the grounds, there's no other opportunity to exercise at all. Most of the time we're either sitting in the schoolroom or sitting on the floor of the temple hall. I'd also like to have some barbells or weights to try and build up some muscles, because I haven't got any yet, but I'm not sure if weightlifting would be allowed for a novice.

My monastery has a big school but the monks and novices can only learn Pali and Dhamma there. I think Pali is a waste of time for me, but Dhamma is useful for everybody. I have a certificate for passing an examination in Dhamma studies. I'm proud of that and I've pinned it to my wall, but I doubt whether I'll ever get one for Pali studies. We have to learn Pali five days every week. It's only for a few hours each day, but it's still very boring. The rest of the day I have duties, such as emptying the rubbish bins and sweeping, but nothing too hard, so I don't mind. On one day each week, I study at a special government school where I learn ordinary high school subjects. I'm now in my second year and I enjoy my studies, especially English. I'm top of the class in some subjects and usually get very good grades. Sometimes in the afternoon, all the monks and novices have to chant at funerals. We have a lot of funerals at my monastery and I like doing them because

LITTLE ANGELS

we usually get a gift of money from the dead person. It's not really from the dead person of course; the family gives it to us for him, so that he can have the merit towards a better new life. Sometimes we have three dead people in the monastery at the same time, so then the novices can earn quite a lot, though I've never had more than 200 baht in one week.

We have three special funeral halls called *sala* at the monastery, all different sizes. People usually rent them for a week and they choose the sala depending on how many mourners they expect to attend the funeral, or how much they can afford. If it's going to be a big funeral, with lots of mourners and dozens of monks invited to chant, they choose sala number three because that's the biggest and nicest hall. Funerals in sala three can take a long time – sometimes an hour – because there are usually lots of sermons and speeches to sit through before the monks and novices do their chanting. Those funerals can be quite boring for us, especially if it's a very hot day, but we usually get about 100 baht each from the dead person because they are usually rich, or were. We can always tell if they were rich because they have beautiful coffins and lots of flowers. But we don't accept invitations to chant at funerals just for the money. Sometimes, we get very poor dead people who have just died at the big hospital near to the monastery. Their relatives deliver the body to us in a plastic bag, because they can't afford a nice coffin. Usually, poor people can't pay to rent a sala for seven days, so the body is just put into a plywood box in front of the crematorium oven and nine monks chant briefly before the body is burnt. Those funerals are over in about ten minutes, but even very poor people like to make merit for the dead person, so they usually give the monks a gift, even if it's only 10 baht and a packet of incense sticks. The monks have to accept the money, otherwise the merit wouldn't be made, but they know even 10 baht is a lot of money for some people, so they usually give it back afterwards and just keep the incense sticks. I feel sorry for poor people. Even when they're dead they don't have such a good time as rich people.

Chanting at funerals is the only way I can get money. My parents can't send me any, but I don't need much anyway. There are some things I have to buy for school, like exercise books and pencils, then if I have some money left over I go to an Internet shop to play computer games. I know that's a waste of money and really as a novice I shouldn't play computer games, but I enjoy them very much. I think all young boys do. Once, a lay-woman told the abbot she'd seen me in the Internet shop, so the abbot scolded me, but he's very old and I don't think he really knows what the Internet is, so he wasn't too hard on me.

I'm very happy to be a novice monk, most of the

time anyway, and I'm glad now that my father suggested it. Being a novice has given me opportunities I wouldn't have had if I'd stayed in my village. I'd probably just be working in the rice fields if I lived at home, but I think being a novice is much better because I can study for my high school diploma. It's also not such hard work and nobody tries to persuade me to take drugs, which I might be doing by now if I was still in the village. I have many good friends amongst the other novices, I can study free and I don't have to worry about food and clothes or bother my parents for money. Because my parents are so far away, being on my own and having to make my own decisions has also helped me to become independent.

Sometimes, when I see ordinary boys wearing nice clothes, or talking with girls, I think I'd like to disrobe so I can be like them and do the things they like to do, especially playing football. Sometimes I talk with the local girls who hang around the monastery grounds, but they're not very interested in football. Monks and novices can only talk to girls if there's a group of us, in case we might be tempted to misbehave or talk about impolite things. We can't sit on the same bench as a girl or touch them in any way. I used to be a bit shy about talking to girls because I don't have hair or eyebrows, but I'm not any more. Really, having cropped hair is very convenient because I don't have to comb it or buy shampoo. Some football superstars shave their heads and very short hair is quite fashionable, so I think girls like it. Anyway, I shouldn't think about girls too much.

Although I'm usually happy as a novice, I'm not going to become a monk. I don't know when I will disrobe, but I can't decide about my future for a few more years, until I finish sixth grade of high school and get my diploma. After that I'm not sure what I'll do. I'd like to carry on studying, perhaps a computer subject at technical college. My parents don't really have any spare money and probably couldn't pay for me to go to college, but I don't need to think about that yet. If I can't study, I'll try and find a good job so I can send money to my parents. If I can't find a job I'll probably just go back to the village and work on the land. I won't mind that too much. My parents are very poor, but at least they can feed me and look after me properly. Some of my novice friends aren't as lucky. Some of them had parents who beat them up or didn't take care of them very well, so they never want to go home again.

Whatever happens to me in the future, I'll never forget my time as a novice monk, even when I'm very old. The life of a novice can be quite difficult for an ordinary boy like me and I think it takes a special kind of boy to be a really good novice. But even an ordinary boy like me can learn a lot, if he does the best he can, and I'm sure living as a novice has improved my behaviour and character. I know I don't always follow the precepts very well, but I try. I haven't had any more ghosts chasing me, so I can't be too bad. At least as a lay-person I'll only have five precepts, which are a lot easier to keep and I wouldn't have to worry about not eating in the evening or some of the other things novices can't do. Besides giving me the opportunity to study, I hope that having lived for a time as a novice and learning Dhamma will help me in the future to be a kind, generous and loving person. I think it will.

5

Novice Banchar

Overcoming the horrors of the past

I've never told anybody my story before. I've always been too ashamed about some of the things I've done and of the things that happened to me. But I've been a novice for a few years now and the Buddha's teaching has helped me come to terms with my past. I still have shameful and unhappy memories but I believe from the moment I became a novice I was reborn, or was at least given a fresh start on a new and better path. I hope when you read my story you won't think too badly of me, or of my sister and mother. We were victims of our circumstances and of an evil and vicious man.

As far as I know, I was born in a Karen hill-tribe village in Chiang Mai province, in the far north, but I believe my mother probably left the village when I was a baby. I can remember an old lady telling me that when I was very young, but I'm not sure if it's true. The old lady lived in the next shack to us, in the shantytown where I spent the first years of my life. The old lady said I didn't look like a full Karen, but she thought my older sister did. She told me that we moved in next to her when I was a new baby, but that I wasn't born there. I know from the way my mother sometimes dressed and spoke that she was from the Karen people, but I have no memories of living in a hill-tribe village. My mother never talked about her home or family and I don't know who my father was.

Although there were about thirty shacks and quite a lot of people, ours wasn't a real village; it was just a slum for destitute people who had nowhere else to go. Most of the people who lived there collected rubbish, like plastic water bottles, tins and cardboard, which they sold to merchants in the town for recycling. The slum was dirty, smelly and always muddy. Many of the people were alcoholics, drug addicts and prostitutes.

My earliest memory of that place is when I was about four or five years old. I remember my sister and I huddling together as rain poured through the roof of our shack, turning the earth floor to mud. In the cool season, when the nights can be very cold in the north, my mother would light a fire in a big tin can to try and keep us warm. Our shack was just one room a few metres square, made from bits of old wood and sheets of tin banged together, with some cardboard for the floor. There was no electricity, no water and no bathroom. We had to get water for drinking and washing from a single tap that served all the shacks. I remember that on the wall of our shack was a small crucifix with an image of Jesus. The crucifix scared me a little, but I didn't really know who or what it represented then. My mother often knelt in front of it to pray and sometimes my sister did as well. I know now that many Karen are Christian, so I think my mother was too.

My sister was about four years older than me. We loved each other very much and I doubt if I would have survived the first few years of my life without her. I suppose my mother must have loved me too, but mostly she ignored me. Usually my sister looked after me, but I know she enjoyed that. Really, my sister was more like a mother to me than my real mother. My sister always promised that some day we would live in a nice house, like ordinary people. She said we would always stay together and we would be happy, like a real family. I looked forward to that very much. When the rain poured through the roof, I sometimes asked her when we would move to our new house.

My sister and I often had very little food and some-times none at all. Usually we ate packets of instant noodles, tins of fish, or whatever we could beg from others. My mother sometimes got money from work-ing in Chiang Mai and then we had better food for a few days. She would take the bus to the city in the evening and maybe wouldn't come home for several days. That didn't matter, because my sister always took care of me and I preferred it when our mother wasn't there. If our mother didn't come home and had forgot-ten to leave us any food, the old lady next door would give us a little rice. She always grumbled about having to feed us, because she was just as poor as us and hardly had enough food for herself. She said our mother was a bad woman for not looking after us properly. I don't know if my mother was a bad woman, but she was quite young and I think she may have been very sad with the way her life had turned out. Sometimes I heard her weeping softly at night, or pray-ing to Jesus. If the old lady gave us only a little rice, my sister always gave me her own share because she worried that I was so thin and my health wasn't very good. I was always sick with something or other when I was little.

Sometimes my mother dressed in traditional Karen clothes and went to the night market in Chiang Mai. She had a big bag of Karen crafts, like beaded hats and bags, which she tried to sell to tourists. She never made those things herself; she bought them from another Karen woman. When my mother went to the night market, she usually took my sister and me. We were always excited about going because the market was such a busy place and so noisy and colourful. There were always crowds of tourists and foreigners and they were fascinating to us. At the market, my mother would lay her goods out on a cloth on the pavement and wait for the tourists to stop and look at them. Sometimes I heard her talking to other Karen women in the market, using a language I couldn't understand. When we went to the market, my mother told my sister and me to wander around the streets and ask foreigners for money. She said we should try to steal things from them and from the market stalls, if we could do it without getting caught. My sister told me that was a bad thing to do and I was frightened of the police, but I became quite clever at stealing small things. I'm sorry about that now. There were many other children doing the same and the traders were very wary of us. When we begged for money, sometimes foreigners gave us a few baht, but usually they pretended not to see us and just walked by.

I remember one time, when I was about five or six, a young foreign woman with long blonde hair gave me ten baht. She smiled and talked to me, but I couldn't understand her. Then she took my hand and led me to a T-shirt stall, where she let me chose a shirt for myself. I chose one with a picture of the badge of Manchester United football club on the front. I didn't know what Manchester United was then, but I liked the colours. I'd never had a new T-shirt before and I thought it was the most wonderful thing that had ever happened to me. After she gave me the T-shirt, the lady took a photograph of me wearing it, then she walked off, smiling and waving to me. I followed her but she caught up with her friends and they told me to go away. I've never forgotten that T-shirt or the lady's kindness. Sometimes I wonder if she looks at her photograph and remembers the little boy she met in Chiang Mai night market. When I got back to my mother's place on the pavement, I was so proud and excited about my new T-shirt, but she made me take it off and put my old ragged one back on. Then she sold my new T-shirt to another woman.

My sister and I didn't go to school, but every day we had to walk from the slum to the main road to beg money from tourists. The place where we lived was close to many big shops that sold Thai crafts, like woodcarvings, silver and pottery. There were always coach-loads of tourists visiting the shops, so my sister and I had to wait near the coaches, look sad and hold our hands out, hoping the tourists would feel sorry for us; two little beggar children with dirty faces and ragged clothes. Usually the shopkeepers or tour guides chased us away, but sometimes we got a little money.

I was a beggar and thief up to the age of eight or nine, which is when a man visited us at the shack for the first time. My mother said he was my uncle. At the time I believed her, but now I don't think it was true. It doesn't matter anyway. He brought sweets for my sister and me and money for my mother, so we were pleased to see him. He came about once a week and always brought small gifts for us. My sister and I liked him very much and looked forward to his visits. He seemed very loving and always hugged and kissed us, just like a father. We didn't know then what an evil man he was.

Some months after our uncle first visited, he arranged for us to move to a proper village. The old wooden house there was tiny and dilapidated, but it had two rooms and at least the rain didn't come in. After the shack, it seemed like a palace to me. The village was very small and run down, but it was much less of a slum and I was grateful to my uncle for taking care of us. There were only a few people in the village. They were all very poor and most of them were quite old, but I enjoyed living there for a time, even though there were no boys of my own age and I didn't have any friends.

I must have been about ten when my mother said I should go to primary school. I'd never been to school, so I was both excited and nervous at the prospect. My uncle didn't stay at the house all the time, but he visited often and he arranged for me to go to a special school not far from the village. It wasn't a real school made of concrete; it was just a sort of wooden barn in a field, especially for children from poor families who lived nearby. I had to walk several kilometres there and back, but I enjoyed studying from the very first day, though I was older than most of the other children in my class. My uncle gave me a school uniform, with a satchel to put my books and lunch in. The uniform was second-hand but I looked very smart and I was so proud of myself. I was especially pleased with the shoes, which were new. I'd never had a pair of shoes before and found it very odd walking in them at first. I've never forgotten that first pair of shoes. When my mother saw me dressed in my uniform on the first day of school, she hugged me and had tears in her eyes. That was the only occasion I can remember her showing any affection for me at all. I've always tried to hold on to that memory.

After we moved, my mother stopped going to the night market to sell Karen crafts but she was away from home more often. Sometimes she didn't come back for a week or more, but my sister was happy to play mother and take care of the house. She wanted to go to school too, but my uncle said it wasn't necessary for a girl to have an education and he wouldn't allow it. He said he was going to arrange for my sister to work in Chiang Mai, so she wouldn't have time to go to school anyway. But my sister wanted to learn and loved looking at my schoolbooks. Each evening, after school, I taught her whatever I had learned that day. She learnt much faster than me and I thought it wasn't fair that she couldn't go to school too. She was a clever girl and even learned to say a few words in English.

I think that was a happy period for me, the only one I can remember, but soon after I started going to school my sister began to change. I thought she was lonely and missed me because I was at school all day, but it wasn't that. She became very unhappy and cried often and she started to hate our uncle. Sometimes he would arrive unexpectedly and stay for a few days, usually when my mother was away. If my sister knew he was coming she would hide in the fields and try to avoid him, as though she was frightened of him. I didn't understand why at the time, because my uncle always brought us small presents and I liked him. Things seemed to have become better for all of us since he came into our lives. We had a nicer house, more food, I was going to school and my mother had regular work. But my sister told me he was *jai dam* – black hearted

– and sometimes she wished we were back in the slum. One time, she told me she wished she was dead, which made me very upset because I couldn't think of anything worse than being without my sister.

Usually, when I walked back from school, my sister would meet me halfway so we could walk together, or play in the fields before going home. One day she didn't meet me. When I arrived home she wasn't there and all her things had gone. My mother was arguing with my uncle, who'd been staying with us in the house for about a week. When I asked my mother where my sister was, she began to cry and became almost hysterical. My uncle was drunk and he shouted at me until I ran out of the house. I looked everywhere for my sister, thinking she was hiding because of the argument, but then a neighbour told me that my uncle had sent her away with some agents to work in a factory in Bangkok. The agents used to come to the villages in our area to find young girls to work in factories in the city, making shoes, clothes and jewellery. That's what they claimed, anyway. They paid the parents quite a lot of money and promised that the children would be taken good care of. I was broken-hearted. My mother didn't seem to love me and now my sister was gone. I sat in a field and cried for hours, convinced I would never see my sister again.

My uncle started to spend more time living at our

house but he and my mother argued and fought constantly. He was usually drunk, even early in the morning, and when they argued he would sometimes slap my mother's face. That upset me and one time I tried to stop him, so he hit me instead. My nose started bleeding, but I'm not very big and I was quite thin then, so I couldn't really defend myself. After that, I realised my sister was right and I started to dislike my uncle. When he was drunk, he usually became violent and beat me often, for no real reason at all. He would hold me by the hair and slap my face, twist my arm behind my back, or beat my backside and legs with a stick. I had bruises from his beatings sometimes, but my mother never really tried to stop him. I became very afraid of him and I realised my mother was too, but he had a hold over both of us. Besides taking care of us, I thought then that the house we lived in was his. I was worried that if I caused a problem, he would send my mother and me back to the slum and I wouldn't be able to go to school. I would probably have to go back to begging and stealing. I loved studying and would rather put up with the beatings than leave school. I decided that when my uncle beat me, I shouldn't try to resist.

Sometimes, on the rare occasions when he wasn't drunk, my uncle could be almost pleasant to my mother and me, but there was usually some other reason for it.

When I was about twelve, he gave me a bicycle so I could ride to school instead of walking. It wasn't new, but I was very pleased to have it. I thought the bike was just to help me get to school, but I soon discovered the real reason my uncle had given it to me. Every Friday evening when I got back from school, he gave me a sealed envelope and I had to ride to a nearby town, about five kilometres away. I had to go to a particular house and give the envelope to a woman who lived there. I always had to go to the back door. She would go into the house, close the door, and then come back with a small package for me to deliver to my uncle. I always had to wear my school uniform and put the package in my satchel. My uncle told me that before I went to the woman's house, I should look up and down the street to make sure nobody was watching.

I could tell from squeezing the package that it contained pills, so I knew my uncle was buying amphetamines to sell to other people. I think he wanted me to wear my uniform so I wouldn't look suspicious when I collected them. Many young people in the nearby villages took drugs, even a few children younger than me. At school I'd been taught that drugs were bad and I didn't want to be involved in my uncle's business, but I had no choice. I was always frightened of going to that house in case the police arrested me. One time when I got to the house, there were two policemen outside. I didn't stop, but as soon as I got round the corner I fell off my bike with fright. I rode straight back home and when I told my uncle about the policemen he became very angry and hit me, even though I hadn't done anything wrong. That was the last time I had to go to that particular house, but I often had to deliver small packets to people in other villages, or sometimes collect money from them.

When I was about thirteen, my mother became sick. She'd been taking amphetamines for a long time, but I knew she'd started taking other drugs too, because I saw her needles and syringe. She became very thin and was always tired. She spent most of the day in bed, but when she wasn't feeling too ill my uncle made her go into town to work. Even though my mother rarely spoke to me, I felt very sorry for her and hated my uncle even more. My mother was ill for nearly a year and then had to go into hospital. She was there for a few weeks, but my uncle wouldn't let me visit her. Then he told me she was dead. He wouldn't let me go to her funeral and I didn't even know where or when it was. I cried a lot when my mother died, but I think I was crying mostly for me, not for her. I felt very lonely.

After my mother died, my uncle went away for a few weeks and I was left in the house alone. I hadn't finished school but sometimes I didn't bother to go. There seemed no point, so I just stayed at home feeling depressed. My mother's crucifix was on the wall and sometimes I knelt in front of it to pray, but I didn't really know what I was supposed to say. I didn't pray for anything important, like the nice house my sister had promised us. I just prayed for my life to get better and for my beatings to stop, and for someone to help me know what to do. I especially prayed that Jesus would keep my sister safe. I asked one of my teachers about Jesus. He told me that Jesus was a kind man who lived in Heaven and loved everybody and took care of them. I asked him why Jesus didn't love me and hadn't taken care of my sister and I. He said it was because we weren't real Christians. I didn't know how to be a real Christian, so I stopped praying.

An old lady who lived nearby was very kind to me at that time. She had her four young grandchildren living in her house, but their parents were working in Bangkok. Every day, she gave me some rice and vegetables and tried to look after me, but she said she was too poor to take care of me all the time. She told me that the house I lived in belonged to one of her sons, who was in prison. She said that I would have to leave because my uncle hadn't paid the rent for weeks. She suggested I should go to a monastery and live there as a temple boy. She knew my uncle beat me often and I think she wanted to get me away from him. Our little village didn't have a monastery, but there was one in a larger village nearby and she took me there. I was nervous, because I'd never been in a monastery before. The abbot was very old, but he seemed to be a gentle and kind man, I think the kindest I'd ever met. He gave me some cake and a fizzy drink and asked me many questions about my family. I couldn't answer most of them. He said that because I had nobody to take care of me, I could stay at the monastery. He suggested I become a novice monk after I finished my primary school studies.

I left the house the next day and moved into the monastery. There were three young novices and one other temple boy living there. They were very friendly to me, so it was better than being in the house on my own. I shared a tiny room with the other temple boy, but I was happy to be with someone of my own age. I didn't really know anything about Buddhism, but the novices explained it to me and I thought it must be a good life, to be a novice monk. I thought I could settle down in the monastery and finish my primary studies, but after about a week my uncle unexpectedly turned up. He told the abbot that he wanted me to go and live in his house, which was in a village about ten kilometres away. I didn't want to go with him but the abbot said I had no choice, because he was my uncle. I told the abbot I didn't think the man was my real uncle, but he still said I had to go with him. I was very unhappy then, and frightened of what the future might bring.

My uncle had a motorbike and he took me to his house. I was surprised that it was quite new and made of concrete, but it was very dirty and untidy inside, with empty whisky bottles everywhere. A young woman sometimes stayed in the house but she never once spoke to me. My uncle said she was his wife, but usually she wasn't there. One time, I found some photographs of her sitting on a beach with an old foreign man. My uncle said that if I lived at his house he would look after me and I could go to school, but in return I would have to work for him in his business. I told him I didn't want to buy and sell drugs because it was a bad thing to do and I was frightened of going to prison. My uncle told me I was already a drug dealer, because I'd made collections and deliveries for him. He said that if he told the police, they would lock me away for many years. I was scared of being sent to prison, so I promised I would do whatever he wanted. I hated staying at my uncle's house. He was drunk nearly every day and quickly became violent for the smallest reason. He would beat me and call me horrible names, or say bad things about my mother and sister, which sometimes made me cry. I didn't understand about such things then, but I realise now that he was probably a sadist, because I'm sure he enjoyed hurting me. My life was horrible, but I had nobody who loved me and I had nowhere else to go.

After I'd lived there for about a year, my uncle came home very drunk one evening. Unusually, he talked to me in a friendly way. He hugged me and told me that he loved me like a son. He gave me a glass of whisky to drink. I'd never drunk alcohol before and I didn't want it, but I drank it because I was so frightened of my uncle. It made me feel sick. He also gave me a pill to take and he said it would make me feel happy. I was afraid he would beat me if I didn't take the pill and he watched to make sure I swallowed it. Later, his friendly mood changed. He told me he had decided to send me to Bangkok with the agents. I cried and begged him not to. He said that maybe he would change his mind, but only if I did everything he told me to. I promised I would. That night, he forced me to do something very disgusting.

Later that night, I didn't cry. I hated my uncle too much to cry. I hated my life and I hated myself. I knew I had to make a new start in my life, because my future looked too terrible. I couldn't stay with my uncle, but I didn't know how to get away from him and didn't know where else to go. I thought about killing him with a big knife from the kitchen. I would have done it, but I didn't want to start my new life by going to prison. I decided to run away, even though I had nowhere to go and nobody to run to. I thought about the people I had known in the past who had been kind to me and who might help me. There was nobody really, but then I remembered the nice old abbot and decided to try and get back to his monastery. I waited until my uncle was asleep and I crept out of the house.

The road was pitch black and I was very scared of ghosts, but I was more scared of not getting away. Every time I heard a noise in the trees, or a dog bark, I jumped in fright. I felt weak and ill and had to stop several times to be sick. I wasn't even sure if I was walking in the right direction, but any road that took me away from my uncle seemed like a good one. It was the right road and I eventually arrived at the monastery. It was still dark and nobody was up. I'd walked a long way, about ten kilometres, and I was very tired. I crawled into a small space under one of the buildings and slept. The chickens and temple dogs woke me up at dawn. When I looked out of the space, I saw the abbot and a few monks leaving the monastery to walk on alms round. I crawled back into the space to wait for them to come back.

When the abbot returned, I went to his kuti. I wasn't sure if he could remember me, so I told him I was an orphan and lived with my uncle, but that he was a very bad man. I told the abbot that my uncle made me sell drugs and wanted me to take them, and that he often beat me. I showed him the bruises on my back and legs. I didn't tell the abbot about the other thing, because I was too ashamed. The abbot told me to have breakfast with the novices while he thought about what he should do. I was worried that he might call the police and have me returned to my uncle, or even arrested. He must have seen I was frightened, so he promised he wouldn't talk to anybody about me.

The novices remembered me. They cheered me up a lot with their chatter and stories about life in the monastery. I envied them because they seemed so happy and carefree. They wanted to know why I had left my uncle, but I just said we had a fight. I fell asleep for a long time after breakfast, then a novice woke me up and told me to hide because my uncle was in the monastery, talking with the abbot. I was so frightened I ran out of the room and went back to my hiding place under the building. It was only when I was in the small space that I realised I could easily be seen from the doorway of the abbot's kuti. After a couple of minutes, two of the novices came casually walking by with a big sheet of corrugated tin. They laid it against the entrance to the space and walked away. I could see out of a crack and I watched my uncle come out of the abbot's kuti, looking angry. He stared around the yard for a few minutes and even walked within a few feet of my hiding place, then he got on his motorbike and drove away. I waited a while and then came out of my hiding place, and my good novice friends said I was to go to the abbot's kuti.

The abbot told me that my uncle had said I was a very bad boy, that I took drugs, stole his money and always told lies. I denied it, but the abbot told me not to worry. He said he believed me and thought my uncle was an evil man. He said he wouldn't send me back to him. I was so relieved I burst into tears. The abbot said I shouldn't stay at his monastery in case my uncle came looking for me again. He said he would telephone his friend, who was the abbot of another monastery far away, and that I should go there to stay. I had never travelled more than a few kilometres on my own, so the abbot said he would send a novice with me.

Later that day, a man with a car took the novice and me to the bus station in Chiang Mai. I was frightened in case my uncle was looking for me there, so I hid in a toilet until it was time to get on our bus. I wasn't sure where we were going, but the novice told me it was a city called Nakhon Sawan. When we arrived early the next morning, we went to a very big monastery and the novice took me to the abbot's kuti. The abbot was very friendly and talked to me like a father. He said that because my parents were dead, I could ordain as a novice monk and live at the monastery. He explained the ten novice precepts to me and warned me that he expected me to be perfectly behaved as a novice. I promised I would be. He said I would have to study at the monastery high school and, if I wanted, I could become a monk when I was old enough. I ordained as a novice the next day. I thought with no hair or eyebrows, and wearing the robes of the novice, my uncle wouldn't recognise me, even if he found out where I was.

I didn't really know anything about Buddhism then, but I soon learned. I grew to love the Buddha for giving me a sanctuary from my problems and for teaching people like monks to be such good, kind men, and so compassionate and understanding about other people's suffering. The Buddha lived such a long time ago, but the monks have never forgotten his teaching. I worked very hard at my studies and learned a lot about Dhamma. For the first time, I felt that I had some direction in my life. I also started going to high school, even though I hadn't quite finished my primary certificate. In my first few months, I had some bad dreams and sleepless nights, but after a while I became happier and started to forget about my past, although I never forgot my sister.

I'd lived at the monastery for more than a year when the abbot sent for me. I thought I was in trouble, but I couldn't think why because I'd tried to be a good novice and to keep all the precepts. The abbot told me he was sorry, but he had some sad news for me. He said his friend, the old abbot from the village monastery, had telephoned and asked him to tell me that my uncle was dead. He'd been stabbed in a drunken fight. I just stared at the abbot. I think he must have forgotten the circumstances that had brought me to his monastery and probably thought I was shocked with grief. He started to gently explain the Buddha's teaching of how everything and everybody are impermanent, and that everything that is born must die. But I wasn't shocked with grief; I was overwhelmed with relief. That day was my seventeenth birthday.

About eight months later, I did have a shock. I was looking out of a schoolroom window on the second floor and saw a foreign man standing in the yard, surrounded by excited little novices. He was laughing, then he waved at somebody I couldn't see. A beautiful young Thai woman came around the corner and walked towards him, smiling. She happened to glance up at my window, though she couldn't see me. My legs went weak and I nearly collapsed on to the floor when I recognised her. It was my sister. I ran downstairs, but then just stood in the doorway to the school, shaking and hardly able to breathe. She saw me and cried my name, then ran across the yard. She couldn't hug me because I am a novice, so we just stared at each other, neither of us able to say anything, but both of us with tears streaming down our faces.

The three of us sat on a bench in the monastery gardens and talked for hours. My sister told me that she'd been looking for me for weeks and had finally been told where I was by the old abbot in the village. Both of us had bad memories from the past that we didn't want to talk about, so mostly we talked of the future. Her friend was German and he was quite a bit older than my sister. He'd been her friend for a year and he seemed a very nice man. She told me she hoped to go to Germany and that they were going to be married. The man couldn't speak much Thai, but to my amazement my sister talked to him in German. The man smiled all the time and I felt he was a good person and that he loved my sister very much. She said they were having a problem about getting a visa for her to live in Germany, because she didn't have the right papers, but they thought they could sort it out. She told me her friend had a nice house in Germany and owned a restaurant there. He planned to open a new Thai restaurant, which my sister would manage. They said they would like me to live with them in their house in Germany after they were married. My sister smiled when she told me that, and I think she remembered her promise to me when we were little children living in the slum.

About a year later, my sister went to Germany and she was married. I think she is very happy and she will visit Thailand soon. She sometimes writes to ask me to disrobe and go to live with her and her husband, but I don't think I can do that. There's something I have to do here. I've read about a monastery just outside Bangkok that takes care of many young children from destitute backgrounds, or who have been abused or neglected in some way. When I finish my high school studies, I'll remain as a novice until I am twenty, then ordain as a monk and go to stay at that monastery. I want to try to help some of those children. Life has taught me about *Dukkha*, suffering, but the Buddha has taught me about love and compassion and how to overcome suffering. That's something I think I can pass on to those unhappy children.

6

Novice Nares

Living with a good heart

The one thing I'll never forget from my child-hood is the image of my parents shouting at each other, and of my angry father hitting my mother. It frightened me. I was only about ten years old and it made me sad and confused that my parents didn't seem to love each other. Their arguments and fights became more frequent as I got older. My father was usually a very kind man, so I couldn't understand why he sometimes acted in such a way. I'm older now, nearly nineteen, and I realise that the difficulties and disappointments of his life must have made him very frustrated and bitter inside. Rice farming is a hard and uncertain life. No matter how much effort you put in, the harvest can easily be ruined by drought or flood, and there's nothing you can do about it.

Even when everything went right, my parents didn't earn much money from their rice farm. There were six of us in the family, so if anything went wrong my father had to borrow from the farmers' community bank. That usually just made things worse later, when the money had to be repaid. The interest mounted up and I think my parents were always in debt. They worried all the time about money and I suppose it was because their lives were so difficult that they argued and fought so often. I understand that now. My parents separated when I was twelve.

Things at home weren't always bad between my parents, especially if we had a good rice harvest. I know they loved me and my older brothers and sister, and we were usually happy together. I think I had a good childhood. I can remember when I was a small boy having lots of good times and adventures with my brothers and the other village boys. Our village is in Nakhon Sawan Province, in the northern region of Thailand. The province is famous because it has the largest lake in Thailand, called Bung Boraphet. During the rainy season, when the lake is full, it covers about 120 square kilometres. Many rare species of crocodiles are bred there in a conservation centre, but there aren't any crocodiles in the lake itself any more.

Sometimes, I'd go to the lake with my brothers and other village children for a day's outing. We would swim, fish and sometimes take a rowing boat out to one of the islands. There wasn't much to do in the village but we liked to ride the buffaloes in the fields, or hunt small animals in the forest with our catapults. I must have killed hundreds of birds and I'm sorry about that now, because it was just for fun and wasn't necessary. It was a cruel thing to do but I didn't understand that when I was young because I hadn't started learning the teaching of the Buddha. Catching fish was to get food for the family to eat, so I'm not ashamed about that.

When I was very young, there was always sufficient food to eat at home. My mother wasn't a particularly good cook and our food was quite plain but there was always enough for a little boy. I usually just had rice and vegetables, sometimes with meat or fish if we could catch any. Things seemed to get gradually worse as I got older. Sometimes we didn't have as much food, though we were never as badly off as some of the other families in the village, who had less land or more children. There was less money for food because my parents had to pay the school expenses for my brothers and sister, which was difficult for them. I think we became quite poor, but the whole village was in a similar position; just about surviving. We accepted that as the way things were for rural people. Nobody in the village had a car or telephone, and some families couldn't afford to use electricity, even though they were connected to the mains supply. Most of the families were heavily in debt. Because all the seventy families in the village were equally poor, I don't think I understood what poverty really was because I couldn't compare our lives with anyone else's. I didn't understand about poverty until somebody gave us an old television, then I saw how some other Thai people lived, especially in the cities. After that, I became quite discontented with my life.

On television, everybody seemed to be rich and always happy in their big houses in Bangkok, with their expensive cars, mobile phones and beautiful clothes. I was very envious of them. I thought people needed those things before they could be happy, so I wanted them for my family and for myself. I think I even started blaming my parents for our poverty and because I didn't have things like a motorcycle or a computer. I started to think my parents had failed their children because they couldn't give us nice things, and because we lived in an old wooden house. Now I know that was a childish idea and I understand that real happiness isn't anything to do with the things you own or where you live. A mobile phone may be convenient, but it can't make you happy or content in any real sense. Since I became a novice, I've learned that genuine happiness and contentment come only from inside, from your own mind. They can't be bought, no matter how wealthy you are. The Buddha taught me that, but I learned it from my own experience too.

If life had sometimes been difficult when my father lived at home, it got much harder after he left. My brothers and sister were living at home when my parents separated, but soon after they moved away from our little village to look for work in the cities, even though they had little education. Only my mother and I were left at home. Most of the young people in the village left as soon as they were able to. Everybody thought they could get rich by going to work in Bangkok, even if they had no qualifications. I think that's just chasing dreams and isn't realistic. One of my brothers soon got into trouble in Bangkok and ended up in prison.

I'd just started at junior high school when my father left home. My primary school was close to the village but the high school was quite far away. I could study at the school free for the first three years but after my father left my mother had a struggle to find the money to pay the other expenses. Usually I had to walk to school and sometimes my mother wasn't able to give me even a few baht to buy food for lunch. My mother was quite desperate for money, but I think I only realised how desperate she was after I had a small accident. On my way home from school one day, I stopped to have a ride on a buffalo in a field, but I fell off into the mud. My school shorts were covered in mud and buffalo dung so I went to a nearby canal, took them off and tried to scrub them clean with a stone. The material was already very thin round the backside because they'd been handed down from brother to brother for years. The stone ripped the cloth. They were ruined and I thought my mother was going to be angry with me. When I got home and showed her the shorts, she wasn't angry, but she looked as though she might cry. She simply didn't have the money to buy another pair. She was very embarrassed that she had to go to a neighbour and beg for a pair of her son's old shorts for me. I felt so sorry for her.

After the family split up, I had to do a lot of extra work in the fields before and after school, and at weekends. I'm not complaining about that, but it was very tiring for me. My mother had a difficult time in those days, so I always tried to do the work with *jai dee* – a good heart. I think if you do things willingly and with a good heart, they don't seem so difficult. But I couldn't do all the work myself and my mother couldn't employ anybody, so some land was left unattended. By then, I also had quite a problem with severe headaches.

Sometimes they made it difficult for me to work in the sun or do heavy manual work for a long time, but I had to do as much as I could to help my mother, even when I felt really ill.

My headaches started after I fell out of a tree, when I was about seven. I banged my head and was knocked unconscious. Our village was a long way from the nearest clinic and there was no way to get me there, so I wasn't examined by a doctor. I regained consciousness after a few minutes and my parents thought I wasn't hurt, but my headaches began soon after. I stopped eating so much and started to lose weight. I'm so thin now I look like a skeleton. When my head hurts, I'm quite absent-minded and sometimes I get very irritable for the smallest reason. I think the fall may have affected my eyesight too, because my headaches always get worse when I read a lot. I like reading, so I just have to put up with the headaches. They've become part of my life now and there's no point complaining about them.

With my mother's difficult financial position, it was obviously going to be impossible for me to study beyond the third year of high school. After that my mother would have to pay for the lessons, as well as all the other expenses. My mother knew how much I wanted to study and I think she felt ashamed that she couldn't afford a proper education for me. I didn't like to see her unhappy, so I always laughed and told her it didn't matter and that she wasn't to worry about it. But in my heart, it did matter. I really wanted to study to get some sort of qualification for a trade, because I thought I could then support my mother properly and she wouldn't have to work so hard when she was old. I knew I could study to sixth grade free by becoming a novice and going to a monastic high school, but that would have left my mother all alone. She had a few health problems herself and wasn't very strong. I thought she wouldn't be able to cope with all the work on her own. I didn't know what to do for the best. Even though I tried to live each day with a good heart, I became very depressed about my life. I began to understand why my father was sometimes so unhappy and frustrated.

After I finished the third year of high school, I left school and worked in the paddy fields for about a year. I worked willingly but it was very hard work, especially as I had to do most of it myself. I never seemed to have any energy and by evening I was often so exhausted and had such a headache that I just collapsed on to the floor. I was only about fourteen then, but I wondered where my life was going and whether that was all I had to look forward to, every day for the rest of my life. It was quite a depressing prospect. It's not surprising that so many young people in villages turn to drink or drugs.

Some of my friends took drugs and they offered them to me sometimes. I never took them, but I was quite tempted.

At about that time my father returned to the village. He hadn't done very well on his own and found it difficult to get by. At first he just helped me in the fields and didn't live at our house, but eventually he and my mother came to an understanding and he moved back in. They still argued a lot, but at least they didn't came to blows anymore. I think they realised they had to make the best of their situation and help each other, especially as they were both already quite old. With my father back at home and working in the fields, I was able to think about my own future more. I talked it over with my parents. They agreed that becoming a novice and continuing my education would be the best course for me. Even though I could have made their lives easier by staying at home and working in the fields, they were very unselfish in their decision and encouraged me. My father was really a lot more unselfish than I realised at the time. He was having a serious problem with his eyesight, but he didn't tell me about it then because he thought it might affect my decision to become a novice. I'll always be grateful to my parents for their encouragement.

Some other village boys who finished at junior high school at the same time as me weren't so fortunate.

Their parents made them leave school to work in the rice paddies. They had no choice about their futures at all and they'll probably just be buffalo boys for the rest of their lives. Rice farming is a simple and honest life, but it isn't what they wanted or dreamed of. I felt sorry for them. Most of them would have liked to continue studying and some were very clever; much cleverer than me. I'm sure, like me, they would have been willing to become novices just for the opportunity to study further. Some of the boys must have been very unhappy about their situation and as depressed about their futures as I was for a time about my own. But I understand the financial pressures on their parents as well. Education at government schools and colleges isn't expensive in Thailand, but even the low fees are beyond many poor families. Given the opportunity, I expect some of those boys now working in the paddy fields could even have gained university degrees and achieved something worthwhile. Poor people like us have a hard time escaping our poverty, which doesn't seem fair to me.

My parents' encouragement made me determined to do the best I could, for them as much as for myself. After the decision was made, I was excited not only about the idea of studying, but also about being a novice and living in a monastery. I wasn't especially interested in Buddhism then, or no more than most young people, but I thought novice monks probably had a very quiet life, without disturbances. I wanted that so I could concentrate on my studies, but also because of my headaches.

I ordained in the village monastery when I was fifteen. It was a small monastery and the new monks and novices learned only about basic Buddhism from the older monks, so I had no intention of staying there. In fact, I stayed only one day, because I'd heard of a monastery in Nakhon Sawan City that had a good high school. The monastery was about twelve kilometres from my village. That's not far, but there was only one bus each day that went from the city to near my village, then there was a walk of about three kilometres down a dirt track. I knew it would be difficult for me to return home very often. I usually manage it about once every two months, if I have money for the bus and the energy for the walk.

It was only after I moved to the city that I discovered novice monks with a three-year high school certificate could study selected courses at the nearby technical college without paying fees. I think that was a pilot project that had just started running in a few government colleges. Usually, students have to pay fees of about 2,000 baht each term, but the government needed more people qualified in technical skills like engineering and electronics, so they tried allowing novices to study free. That seemed like good thinking to me, but the project has since been discontinued. My own parents could never have afforded to pay the fees for me to study as an ordinary student, so discovering that I could study free was very exciting for me. I'd already decided that I would like to be a computer engineer, though I'm not sure why because at that time I'd never even used a computer. Being able to study at the college as a novice meant that I didn't have to buy the college uniform, shoes or sports clothes, or pay many other expenses that were compulsory for ordinary students. I was also able to live and eat free at the monastery, so I found myself in an ideal situation.

The abbot of my monastery was keen for his novices to study for a skill that they could use in the future. I think he was a wise and realistic man. He knew that most of his novices came from poor families and had ordained just to get some sort of education. He'd come from a similar rural background himself, so he was very compassionate and understanding towards us. He understood we weren't really so interested in being novices, or devoting ourselves to the Buddha's teaching for the rest of our lives, as he had done. At the same time, he was determined that while we were in his care we should at least learn how to live in a moral way. I think he had a good outlook.

I enrolled at the college for a computer course and I've studied there for nearly three years. I enjoy my studies, but the mathematics are difficult and calculus definitely make my headaches worse. When I first started studying, the thousands of students at the college included about thirty novices, all studying free. I'm not sure why, but all except two of the novices dropped out within a year or so. I think that maybe having to live as novice monks, but mixing and chatting all day with ordinary boys, may have been difficult for them. Perhaps it made them unsettled or unhappy with their lives as novices, especially when the other boys talked about their girlfriends or the good times they had after college closed. None of that bothers me, because I can accept my situation as it is. Anyway, I want to get some sort of qualification before I think about having a girlfriend or settling down. Sometimes, the other students tease me a little because I can't do some of the things that ordinary boys like to do, but they don't mean to be hurtful and I have many friends at the college.

The free education for novices is only for an ordinary vocational certificate, given after three years of study. I'd really like to stay on to study for the higher diploma too. Unfortunately, even novices must pay for that extra two years' course and it's quite expensive, so I don't think I'll be able to. My real dream is to go to university and study for a degree. If I had a degree, I would be the only person in my village ever to get one, which would make my parents very proud. I'd like that, because they've given up a lot to help me. But I have to be sensible about my ambitions, otherwise I will only be disappointed if I can't achieve them. I think everybody should have ambition, but we must be realistic and know what's possible, and what isn't. I'll be happy just to get my ordinary certificate and I'm grateful to have that opportunity, which I wouldn't have had if I hadn't become a novice.

Although my abbot wants his novices to study for useful qualifications, that doesn't mean we can behave like ordinary students. Technical college students have a reputation for being rowdy and sometimes get into trouble, but the abbot teaches us how to behave and live properly. I'm a novice monk, living in a monastery, so I have to try to follow the precepts and rules of the novice and balance my studies at the college with my religious life. That's not very easy sometimes, but I try my best because it's my duty and because the abbot is so kind to me.

Because I'm a student as well as a novice, some of the precepts and rules are difficult to follow. I have to pay my bus fare to get to college every day and I have to buy books, so I need to handle money. That's against the novice precepts, but I think we have to be sensible about them, according to our situation. Some of the lay-people who visit the monastery try to help the poor novices by giving them a little money, because they know our parents can't usually send us any. If I have any money to spare, I usually buy books about computers or science, but I like reading cartoon books too, if I have time to relax.

Maybe breaking the precept about money isn't so important these days, and it's unavoidable for me anyway, but sometimes I break other precepts and rules too. I think that's human nature, especially for young boys. The Dhamma teaches us that if we are sufficiently self-disciplined we can rise above ordinary human nature and become something better. I believe that's true, but it's also very difficult for most people to do, including me. When I get back from college in the evening, I'm usually hungry and sometimes I eat some rice. I know that's wrong for a novice, but I'm not really a very strong boy and I think I should be careful about my health. If I don't eat enough food, I always get a headache. But I try my best to be a good novice and not a bad one.

Every time I break a precept, I try to make up for it by doing something good, like sweeping the monastery grounds or helping the old monks, even if I haven't been told to. The point is that I always know for myself when I've broken a precept or rule and I feel a little ashamed about it, so just knowing I've been bad is the punishment for me. Whether I'm successful at following the precepts or not, they've made me much more aware of my own good and bad behaviour. Now I try to think more carefully before I do or say anything and try to be aware of the possible results of my actions or speech. Sometimes, I see other novices and monks behaving badly, much worse than me, but I try not to be influenced by them. I also see others practising really well, but that doesn't influence me either because I think I'm already doing the best I personally can. But I admire them when I see them practising properly and I'm glad there are so many good monks and novices.

Like all the other monks and novices, I get up at about 5am and walk on alms round, and then attend the morning service. Sometimes I think the chanting is a waste of time. It's not interesting but it's part of my duty as a novice and the abbot expects it, so I do it. Besides going to college, I have to study Pali and Dhamma at the monastery school and I also practise meditation. I don't think Pali is much use to me because I don't want to be a monk. We usually just have to learn it by heart, but sometimes without much understanding. I like meditation because I think it's helpful not only in my life as a novice and student now, but will also be useful in the future when I have to work,

119

or have my own family. It trains me to be calm, to keep control of my bad feelings, and it helps my headache go away for a while. After I meditate, my thinking is always clearer, which is useful in my studies. I often meditate late at night but I share a room with four other novices, so sometimes it's difficult to have a peaceful environment.

Learning the teaching of the Buddha has been very beneficial for me. I think everybody should study the Dhamma because it's a good way to live our daily life, especially if we try to follow the Eight-Fold Path, which is the ethical code for Buddhists. The Dhamma encourages me to try to be a good person and to help other people when they have a problem. Most people have the same type of problems, so we should be sympathetic and compassionate when they need our help, even if we don't like them particularly. One day, we might need their help for our own problems. Studying Dhamma has also made me understand why I shouldn't get angry or envious, or carry hatred in my mind, and why I should be careful about how I speak or act, and even think. That's my *kamma* and can affect what happens to me in the future. I want my future to be good, so everything I say or do now has to be good too. That's how kamma works. I think everybody should study the teaching of the Buddha. Even if people are Christian or follow some other religion, they could still benefit from the Buddha's teaching because it's such common sense and so logical.

If my parents could afford to help me study for a higher technical diploma, I'd continue studying at the college. I know they won't be able to, so I have to think about disrobing and looking for a job when my present course ends. I'll probably have to go to Bangkok to get a job, because that's where all the best jobs are. I don't mind that. I'm nearly nineteen, so I would have to think about disrobing soon anyway, or becoming a monk when I reach twenty. I don't want to be a monk yet, though I probably will be for a short time in the future, in my village monastery, just to make merit for my parents. I know my mother would be very happy and proud to see me ordain as a monk, so I should do it for her sake and as a way of thanking her for all she has done for me. My brothers have got their own families now, so they don't have any spare money to help me study further. They try to send money home to my parents whenever they can, but they never did become rich by living in the big city.

I don't think there's any point worrying too much about the future. I believe I can have a happy life whether I study further or not, and no matter what job I eventually get. I've learned a lot while I've been a novice. I know from the Buddha's teaching that we can't always get what we want, but that we should be content with what we can achieve through living our life in a good and moral way. If we can't get what we want, there's no point giving ourselves even more problems by complaining about it or becoming bitter or unhappy about our situation. I think that's something my father never learned. The Buddha has taught me that happiness and sadness come from our own minds, whatever our situation or environment. If we do good things we will be happy and if we do bad things we will be unhappy. That seems logical and I accept it.

Subsequently . . .

Phra Peter was concerned about Nares's debilitating headaches and poor eyesight and arranged for him to be examined by a specialist. An old but treatable condition was diagnosed which was relieved within a few months by a course of drugs. The Students' Education Trust also gave Nares a grant for spectacles, which he badly needed. After thirteen years, Nares's headaches finally stopped.

After gaining his Ordinary Vocational Certificate from technical college, Nares disrobed, intending to look for a job. Because he ideally wanted to study further, he was offered a scholarship by the Students' Education Trust. With the scholarship, Nares continued his studies for two more years at technical college for a Higher Diploma in

Computer Electronics and then, still with SET's support, studied for a university degree in Industrial Management. After gaining his degree, Nares joined the Royal Thai Airforce as a technician. He has since paid off his parents' debts and secured his family's land.

7

Novice Phisarn

Buffalo boy makes good

When I was a young boy, I loved my buffalo more than almost anything else in the world. I think I loved it even more than the little girl who sat next to me at primary school. I was only about nine, but I thought she was beautiful. But my buffalo was beautiful too, in its own way.

My buffalo was a gentle animal with big, sad eyes. It walked very slowly and calmly, never running or making a fuss. Because buffaloes are slow, people think they're stupid and dull, but they're not. They are really quite dignified and noble, and they can learn. They have their own personalities, just like people. My buffalo was never bad-tempered and never bit or kicked me. It worked in the rice fields all day in the sun with my father, pulling a heavy plough. The buffalo must have been quite tired by the end of the day, but it never complained when my friends and I climbed on to its back for a ride after school. It would take us wherever we wanted to go. Usually, we rode it down to a canal near our village. It would squelch through the mud on the banks, walk straight into the water and then just stand there quietly, so we could dive off its back. I think the buffalo enjoyed itself as much as we did, especially when we splashed water over it to give it a wash.

I was about five years old the first time I rode on my buffalo. It seemed so huge to me, but I wasn't frightened because it had been part of my life since I was a baby. I was so small, I could almost walk under its belly without ducking my head, but buffaloes can be surprisingly incontinent so I never did. The first time I rode it, my father put his hands under my arms and gently lifted me on to the buffalo's neck, so I could lean forward and hold on to its long, swept-back horns, screaming with happiness and delight. I felt so grand, sitting on the back of such a huge creature, like a mahout on his elephant!

We had four buffaloes, but that one was my favourite. Thai people don't usually give names to animals and instead refer to them by their colour. My special buffalo had reddish skin, so I called it *Daeng*, which means 'red'. The buffaloes lived under my family's house, which was in a small village in Srisaket province, in the northeast of Thailand.

All the eighty houses in the village were the same; single storey and very old, made of wood with zinc roofs. The floor in my house must have been recycled many times, because it was much older than the rest of the house. It was made of wide, ancient planks, teakwood I think, worn smooth and polished by generations of bare feet. Most houses had just one big room, sometimes partitioned with cupboards or curtains. Cooking was done outside and the washroom and toilet were behind the house. Each house stood on four stilts, about four metres high, which made an open area underneath. The houses were built on stilts so they wouldn't get flooded during the rainy season, and the steep and rickety stairs up to the living area helped keep snakes and other creatures out of the house. Sometimes they got in anyway. In villages like mine, the space underneath the house is used as a pen for animals, because they can live there protected from the sun and rain. Our four buffaloes and two pigs lived in the pen under the house, so it was a very smelly quagmire, with lots of flies and mosquitoes. We get used to that sort of thing in the countryside and it doesn't bother us. I was born in the house, so the very first breath of air I took smelled of buffalo dung. That's the smell of home to me.

When I was a boy, my father told me that the government was trying to persuade farmers to modernise by getting rid of their buffaloes and to buy tractors instead. They said mechanising the farms would make rural people richer. I think few families in our village earned more than about 12,000 baht a year from growing rice, so the idea of having more income was attractive. Some farmers in our village decided to follow the government's advice, but even after selling their buffaloes they usually had to borrow money from the bank to buy the expensive tractors. They just got into a lot of debt and in the long run buying tractors really made them poorer. Tractors need expensive fuel, they pollute the atmosphere with fumes and noise, they break down, wear out, and they don't give anything back to the earth. Buffaloes eat grass, they're strong and rarely get sick, they make hardly any noise and every five minutes they help fertilise the earth. They also make more free buffaloes, so it doesn't seem good sense to me to get rid of them. Some farmers in my village who bought tractors have now gone back to using buffaloes again. It's harder work, but they've realised that the traditional ways are sometimes better for people in their situation, whatever the government says. Probably the idea of mechanisation came from some politician who'd never worked on the land and didn't really understand farmers' problems. I'm glad my father never exchanged our buffaloes for a tractor, because I would have been without my best companion when I was a child.

Even as I got older, when I was about ten, the only thing I wanted to be was a buffalo boy for the rest of my life, to take care of all the buffaloes and ride Daeng every day. I thought there could be nothing better than that. When I finished my primary education, I didn't want to go to high school. I was happy to be free of studying and have so much time to play, though I also had to work very hard in the rice fields every day. Anyway, my two older sisters were already in junior high school and I don't think my parents could afford to send all three of us to study. That was a good thing, as far as I was concerned. For a time, I was happy just working in the fields and I thought that would be my life.

After I finished primary school, I know I became a bit wild and difficult for my parents to handle. I was always up to mischief; usually nothing too bad, but serious enough that my father sometimes had to take a stick to me. He was quite fair and would just warn me the first time, but if I did the same thing again I would get a hard beating. I always deserved it, so I can't complain. I was never in trouble with the police, but I once did a very bad thing which I later became extremely ashamed about. I've never forgotten it and probably never will, but I learned an important lesson.

My mother used to hide a small amount of money on top of a tall, glass-fronted cupboard that divided our house into two rooms. There was never more than a few baht up there, but it was all she'd managed to save. One day I wanted to buy sweets, so I climbed up on the cupboard to steal her money. I know that sounds terrible, wanting to steal my mother's money, especially when the family was so poor, but I never thought of it like that. I just knew I wanted to buy sweets for myself. When I was almost on top of the cupboard, it fell over on me with a great crash and I was badly cut by broken glass. I had to go to hospital to have my cuts stitched up. My father was very angry and beat me; the worst beating I ever had. Immediately afterwards, I thought the beating was my punishment, but I realised later, when I began to feel so bad about trying to steal my mother's money, that the shame itself was the real and lasting punishment, even more than my cuts or sore backside. In Buddhism, we learn about the law of cause and effect, or kamma, which says that we always get a good result from our good actions and a bad result from our bad actions. The cuts and beating were the immediate bad results from my action, but the shame has been an even worse and longer lasting result. Even now, years afterwards, I sometimes think of what I tried to do, and I'm still ashamed of myself. I don't think I had much sense of right and wrong then and only really understood after

I started to study Dhamma, when I became a novice. I'm glad I had that chance, or I don't know what sort of person I might have eventually turned into.

Two of my friends were dek wat (temple boys) at the village monastery. They lived there all the time because their parents couldn't afford to look after them at home. That's a very common arrangement in Thailand for poor people. Even one of our former Prime Ministers, Mr Chuan Lekpai, was a dek wat when he was a young boy. My friends had duties to help keep the monastery tidy and to look after the three monks and two novices who lived there. I often helped my friends in their work or played at the monastery and I became quite involved in the life there, though I had no interest in Buddhism. Sometimes I stayed at the monastery all night instead of going home. I think that suited my parents because I was causing too many problems at home.

After I got to know the monks a little, one of them suggested I should think about becoming a novice myself, so I could study. I wasn't at all sure about that. I didn't really want to study anyway and even then, at twelve, I knew monks and novices couldn't do certain things, or at least weren't supposed to. I was already quite interested in girls, though I wasn't really sure why. I told the monk I didn't want to be a novice, but he talked about it with my parents and they thought it was a good idea. I'm sure that was mainly because they couldn't handle me at home any more. My father had been a monk for two years before he was married and he said I might learn some discipline if I ordained. My mother was especially pleased with the idea. She told me that if a son is a monk or novice, the parents are taken to heaven after they die by holding on to their son's robe. I didn't know whether that was true or not, but I liked the idea of making merit for my parents, because I really did love them, even though I caused them so many problems. I finally agreed to become a novice.

I ordained when I was twelve but it was another two years before I really started thinking about studying. By then I'd become very bored with the lazy life I was leading at the monastery. I have to admit, in that first two years I wasn't a very good novice. Well, really, I was a very bad one. I always behaved myself if there were lay-people watching, but as soon as they'd gone I just went back to being like an ordinary boy and getting up to all the usual mischief. I didn't take drugs or drink alcohol anyway, but the other novice precepts didn't concern me at all. I knew them, but I didn't consider myself to be a real novice so I didn't make any effort to follow them. The other novices were the same. I'm sorry about that now.

The only time I enjoyed those first two years was when all the monks and novices walked on *thudong*.

Thudong is like a pilgrimage and is how the Buddha lived his life most of the time, wandering from place to place. We take only the essential things, like our alms bowl and water bottle, and walk into the forest for a few days, sleeping in the open air under a special umbrella called a *glot*. At night, the glot can be hooked on to a tree branch and a mosquito net hung over it, which makes a sort of tent just big enough for one person. On thudong, the monk is supposed to sit up all night in his tent meditating, but for us young novices it was really just like camping and a chance to play in the forest. I'm not sure that the monks really enjoyed it very much either, because they were quite frightened of the ghosts that live in Thai forests.

After a couple of years of living as a novice, I'd got over the idea of being a buffalo boy, but I still saw Daeng every day. Sometimes, if nobody could see, I would take my robes off and ride on him. But by then I was so bored I started to think of what else I could do with my life. I didn't really have any idea at all, but I knew whatever I did I'd probably have to study first. One of the other novices had been caught doing something very bad and had been told to leave our monastery by the Abbot. The novice had moved to another monastery in Nakhon Sawan Province, which was about two hundred kilometres from Srisaket. Only about thirty monks lived at that monastery but there were nearly two hundred novices, as well as a large community of nuns living in a separate compound. Each year the monastery held a special meditation retreat for women, sometimes with more than a thousand temporarily becoming nuns. My friend was studying for his high school diploma in the monastery school, which he said was a very good one. He said he had a lot of fun at the monastery with all the other novices, so I decided to join him there.

I'm glad I made the move, but my home is now so far away that I can visit only once a year, usually only for a few days each time. On the train, the journey takes about nine hours and the fare is expensive. One of my sisters now works in a factory in Bangkok and she usually sends me 200 baht every month, but that's only enough to buy the things I need, like toothpaste and washing powder, so it's hard for me to save money to go home very often. I miss my mother and father a lot sometimes, and I miss Daeng too.

When I first moved to the monastery in Nakhon Sawan, some of the other novices made fun of me because I couldn't speak Thai very well. At home in the village we usually spoke Laos and my Thai wasn't so good. The languages are similar in many ways, but some words and tones are totally different, so my first job was to improve my Thai. It was while trying to do that, and at the same time studying Pali, that I became quite interested in both languages. Many Thai words come from Pali and I found it fascinating to work out how they'd become absorbed into the Thai language and how their original meaning may have changed or been adapted. For the first time, I realised that studying could be enjoyable, especially if you were interested in the subject. I discovered that it wasn't just about filling your head with a lot of useless information, or getting a diploma. But I was proud to get my diplomas too. I did quite well in Pali studies and earned a certificate, as well as one for Dhamma.

Besides learning Pali and Dhamma, I started my six years of high school studies at the monastery, which has its own lay-teachers as well as a few monk teachers. I was surprised at how much I enjoyed studying and I usually manage to get good grades for every subject, except English. I can't cope with English at all, maybe because I'm also learning Pali and Thai but my brain still thinks in Laos. I don't think it can handle so many languages at the same time. One time, in an English test, the students had to listen to a passage about American history and then give written answers to questions about what we'd heard. Part of the passage said, 'Abraham Lincoln was born in a log cabin', but when the teacher asked us where the President was born, I wrote 'Imbraham Bacon was born in a long cabbage'. I got zero marks for the test, but the teacher gave me a couple of marks for making him laugh. I'm still not sure why he thought my answer was funny.

Living at my monastery is good fun sometimes. There are many novices there, so I've lots of friends of my own age. I think the novices fall into three groups: a few are very serious in their practice and want to become monks, a few are very badly behaved, and the majority of us are somewhere in between. I've known of a few novices who've taken drugs, but as soon as they've been caught they've been kicked out of the monastery. A few of the older boys even try to spy on the nuns while they're taking a shower, but I think that's a very bad thing to do. If they're caught, they're also sent away from the monastery. (But some of the nuns are quite pretty, and they're not all old.) Although there are some excellent novices, really interested in Pali and devoted to Dhamma, I think the majority of us just use our time as an opportunity to live and eat free while we study at high school. That was my idea too, until recently. When I ordained I thought if you weren't really serious about being a novice, there didn't seem much point in following the novice precepts. I've changed my ideas now, and I try harder.

Before, when walking on alms round, people would often give me packets of instant noodles or tins of fish, but for breakfast I usually ate the fresh rice and curry they offered. The packets and tins would be sitting on a shelf in my room at night, so if I felt hungry it seemed stupid not to eat them. I didn't even think about the precept. I was hungry, so I ate them. I suppose my attitude hadn't really changed much from a few years before when I tried to steal my mother's money. I just thought about what I wanted and didn't consider whether my action was good or bad. I have to admit, I still eat in the evening sometimes, but only if I'm very hungry or missed my lunch. But now I always say a prayer to the Buddha to apologise. I know that until recently I was quite irresponsible as a novice, but I hope I've changed my outlook in the past year or so. I understand now that the precepts are necessary and important, even for the youngest novices, and that we need the respect of the lay-people. The lay-people provide everything for our lives in the monastery, so we have a duty to behave as they expect, and not just how we want to.

It was in the fourth year of my high school studies when something happened that caused a major change in my outlook. It really got me thinking about the future seriously for the first time, and also about my behaviour as a novice in the present. One of the monk teachers couldn't take his usual Dhamma class of first year novices and he asked me to stand in for him. I'd been a novice for about six years by then, so I thought I'd be able to handle the class of mostly very young novices. I agreed to do it, although I was quite nervous about talking in front of the class.

When I walked into the classroom, all the little novices politely stood up and paid respect to me, calling me *ajahn* (teacher), which was very flattering. Although I was nervous, the students seemed quite relaxed, maybe because I was much younger than their usual old monk teacher. That made me relax too and I found I was able to talk to them in a friendly way that they could understand easily. They sat and listened attentively and seemed genuinely interested in what I had to say. They didn't give me any trouble at all. At the end of the lesson, all the students stood up again and paid respect to me when I left the room, saying they hoped I would teach them the next week too. That was a double Dhamma lesson lasting nearly two hours, but for me the time flew by. At the end of the lesson, I had such a good feeling and realised how much I'd enjoyed teaching the little ones. For the first time in my life, I had the feeling not only of having given something to other people, by sharing what I'd learned, but also of being somebody who mattered and who could make a difference for others. I suppose I felt quite important and realised that even someone like me could earn the respect of other people. I think on that day two things happened to me: I began to grow up and become more responsible, and I discovered what I most wanted to do. I wanted to be a teacher. Maybe that sounds ridiculous to you; a poor, lowly buffalo boy having such an ambition, but I felt quite determined that I could do it.

After that, when I attended my classes I tried not only to listen to what the teachers had to say but also how they said it, how they made what they were teaching sound interesting or important and how they kept control of so many rowdy youngsters. I realised that sometimes the teacher had to be strict, but sometimes he could be light-hearted and friendly if it helped get his points across. I also realised that psychology and an understanding of young people played a big part in teaching well. Some of the teachers didn't appear to be very interested in their job, but others seemed really motivated and obviously enjoyed their work very much. I admired those teachers and wanted to be the same.

I asked the head teacher if I could have a class of my own to teach. He agreed and I now regularly teach classes of young or new novices. I always enjoy it. Sometimes I teach very basic Pali, but usually Dhamma. I think the boys enjoy having me as their teacher as much as I enjoy teaching them. The responsibility of teaching has also given me a better attitude to being a novice. Because I'm their teacher, the little ones look up to me to set an example, so I have to do my best for them by always trying to behave well. I know some of them misbehave just as I used to, but they're only little boys so I try to be understanding towards them. My dream would be to train to be a proper teacher, because I know teaching isn't just a matter of standing in front of students and talking; it's a real skill that has to be learned. I'd like to teach in an ordinary school, but I don't think there's any possibility of that. I'll soon finish my six years of high school, but I'm already nineteen. If I disrobe after I have my high school diploma, there's no way my parents could ever afford to send me to teacher training college for four years, and I don't have any money. I'll have to look for any job I can find, with just my high school diploma. The only way I can be a teacher at all is to remain in the robes and ordain as a monk when I reach twenty. If I did that, I could teach Dhamma and basic Pali in the monastery school, which I know I would find satisfying, but . . .

The 'but' is that I really don't want to be a monk. I've enjoyed my time as a novice, but one of the reasons I've enjoyed it is that until recently I've never taken my life as a novice very seriously, or not as seriously as I now wish I had done. I've broken most of the precepts regularly, though I've never stolen anything or taken drugs. Maybe admitting I've regularly broken most of the precepts makes me sound like a bad boy, but I don't think I am, not inside. Not too bad, anyway. But I'm not cut out to be an *arahant* (Buddhist perfected being) either. I'm just an ordinary boy, with ordinary weaknesses and desires. One of those desires is to do the same things that other young men enjoy. I've always liked girls but I've never had a girlfriend. I've never even held hands with a girl, let alone kissed one. (I did once try to kiss the pretty girl who sat next to me in primary school, but she made a noise like she was being sick and pushed me away. She said I smelt like a buffalo.) I'm not some sort of sex maniac, but I'd like an ordinary relationship with a nice girl and a house and family of my own sometime.

If I became a monk, I couldn't have the same relaxed attitude to the precepts that I've sometimes had as a novice. To me, being a monk is much more serious and more important than just being a novice. It's a completely different thing. I respect monks very much because to ordinary people they represent the Buddha and his teaching. There's nothing more important than that. If I was a monk, I'd have to follow all the 227 precepts strictly and I think that could make a lot of mental conflict for me. I don't think I would be happy in that situation. If I broke a precept – and I think that would be inevitable – I know I would be very ashamed and feel like a 'false monk'. If I wasn't happy as a monk, maybe that would affect my performance as a teacher too.

At the moment, I'm not really sure what to do, but

I still have about a year to decide about my future. I'm quite pleased with my progress in the past few years. I started off wanting to be an ignorant buffalo boy all my life. Now I have certificates in Pali and Dhamma and soon I'll have my high school diploma too, and I'm teaching others. In a small way, people respect me and look to me to set an example. I never envisaged any of that a few years ago and wouldn't even have dreamed it was possible. I don't think the future ever works out how we plan, or how we want it to, so for the moment I'm content to wait and see what happens. Whether I become a proper teacher or not, I know I have in it me to be a good man and to be happy with whatever I do. I'm certainly going to try.

It's a sad coincidence, but while I was helping to write this story I had a letter from my parents to say that my buffalo, Daeng, had died of old age. He'd already lived much longer than usual for a buffalo and in the last few years hadn't been able to work much because he was almost blind. I was very sorry to hear about that. He'd worked tirelessly all his long life, just being a good buffalo, never causing any problem for anybody. After I read the letter, I went to the big Buddha image in the temple hall and lit some candles and incense sticks for the Buddha, from Daeng. I'll never forget how much pleasure we had together when we were both younger; a buffalo boy and his buffalo.

Subsequently:

Phisarn was given a scholarship by the Students' Education Trust and studied for a degree in Public Administration and Law, with a minor in Thai. He is now a research assistant for a university professor but also returns regularly to his old monastic school to teach Thai to young novices.

8

Novice Adisak

'I know who I am and what I am'

Almost from as far back as I can remember, I've wanted to be a monk. I will be soon. I've lived as a novice for nearly four years and I can't imagine any better future than remaining in the robes, I hope for the rest of my life. I'm a happy boy, I try to be a well behaved novice and I believe I can be a good monk. Considering how things might have been, I'm sometimes surprised that my life has turned out so well. I have my mother and the Dhamma to thank for that.

If I hadn't learned Dhamma from my mother when I was very young, and later ordained as a novice, my life could have been a lot different. I'm sure it would be much worse. Although I had to wait until my father died before I could become a novice, when I was sixteen, it was all I really wanted to do from about the age of eight. Even before then, I'd already realised that I was surrounded by bad influences on every side. My father was a drunk and often beat my mother and me. Many of the other village boys, even some not much older than me, were taking amphetamines or sniffing glue or thinners. My little village in Saraburi Province, in the central region of Thailand, was full of thieves and drug dealers. The village was the whole world to me then and it seemed just about everybody I knew in that world was a bad person in one way or another. I was frightened that I might have no choice but to become the same as them as I got older. I was worried and confused about my future and what would happen to me. I think my mother was very worried as well.

My mother is a good, hardworking person. She is also very religious. She's always tried to live her life by the teaching of the Buddha and she taught me to do the same. When I was about ten, she explained the five precepts that the Buddha gave to ordinary people, so I would know what was right and what was wrong, and how I should behave. She helped me understand why I shouldn't kill, steal, lie, take drugs or drink alcohol, although the last was already obvious to me because of my father's drunkenness. I wasn't sure then about the precept concerning wrong sexual behaviour, but I understood that one later. Because my mother had told me that breaking the five precepts was wrong, I couldn't understand why such bad things seemed to be going on all around me every day, and even in my own house sometimes. My mother explained to me that it wasn't Buddhism doing those bad things, it was people doing them, and I shouldn't lose my faith in the Buddha's teaching because others couldn't follow it very well. She said I should always follows the precepts and do what I knew in my heart to be right, regardless of what anybody else did. That was good advice that I've always tried to follow.

My mother wanted me to become a novice as soon as I could. She thought that was the only thing that would protect me and help me live my life in a good way. I thought so too and I very much wanted to ordain, but my father wouldn't allow it. I don't know why, but he was set against the idea. He'd never been a monk or novice himself and I don't think he had a great deal of respect for the Sangha, nor even any interest in Buddhism. I'm sorry he never ordained because if he'd lived as a monk, even for a short time, it might have helped him to be a better person. I think my father didn't want me to ordain because he wanted me to labour in the rice paddies, or get some other job, so he wouldn't have to work so much himself. Whenever I mentioned the subject of becoming a novice, he would fly into a rage and slap my face and then hit my mother for encouraging me. I used to feel very upset when I saw my mother crying after my father hit her. I pitied her for the unpleasant life she had to lead sometimes, but there was nothing I could do to help. In the end, I thought it best to stop mentioning ordaining at all. But the dream never left me.

Perhaps because I was aware of so many bad things going on around me, I developed greater respect for the monks in my village monastery. They seemed to be such good men. As a child of seven or eight, I would offer rice to them every day as they walked by our house on alms round. After I put the rice in their bowls, the monks would bless me and I felt their blessing kept me safe for the day. Once each week, on Wan Phra, the monks didn't walk on alms round, so then I would go to the monastery and offer food to them there. I enjoyed that very much; seeing the monks sitting on their mats looking so calm and dignified. They inspired me to resist the temptations that other people, even my best friends, seemed to be trying to put in my way all the time.

Sometimes, when all your friends are behaving in a certain way, even when you know it's a bad way, it can be difficult to resist doing the same, especially when you are young. Everybody wants to be accepted by the crowd and be part of the group, so it was quite difficult to refuse when my friends tried to get me to take amphetamines, sniff glue or thinners, smoke cigarettes or drink whisky. My friends used to tell me it was the smart thing to do, and good fun. They told me I wouldn't be the same as them if I didn't do it. But I didn't want to be the same and I didn't think it was smart at all, though I never said so. I never did any of those things, but if I hadn't ordained as a novice, perhaps they would eventually have persuaded me. Sometimes, when I go home to my village, I still see some of the boys who used to be my friends. They are all about nineteen or twenty now, but they are completely addicted to alcohol and drugs. One amphetamine pill costs about eighty baht in my village and some of them take pills every day. They can't earn that much money from working in the rice paddies, so I know they have to steal, sell drugs to other people or commit other crimes to get money. A few of them already have young families and I can see how their wives and children suffer from drunken violence, or not even having enough food to eat. A couple of my old friends are in prison already.

Despite the difficulties I sometimes had at home, I was mostly happy as a child. I especially enjoyed being with my mother and helping her in her work. She sold food from a roadside stall. Every morning at 5am, we went to the market together to buy fresh vegetables, pork and chicken. Thai people like to bargain for nearly everything. I was quite good at it and enjoyed getting a lower price than the market traders asked. It made me proud that I was able to help my mother save a few baht here and there. On our way home from the market, I would excitedly replay my bargaining with the traders word for word and tell my mother how clever I'd been to get 10 baht off the price of a chicken. She would always laugh and praise me then, which made me very happy because she never laughed much when my father was around. When we got back from the market, I'd help her cook the food before I went to primary school. Her little stall sold pork balls on sticks, noodles and chicken fried rice and it had a few tables and chairs on the street, like an outdoor restaurant. A bowl of food on my mother's stall was only twelve baht so she didn't make a lot of money, but we weren't as poor as some other families in the village.

My mother was careful with her money and she was never in debt. I think she earned about 200–300 baht a day, but she had to buy fresh food for the next day from that, so only about half of it was profit. My father drank most of the profit away. But it didn't really matter to us that we didn't have much spare money because my mother and I knew that she was earning money in a good way, honestly, and through her own hard work. She was content because she was following the Buddha's teaching about 'Right Livelihood', which is part of the

Eight-Fold Path for ethical behaviour. The Path covers every aspect of our behaviour and if we follow it we can't go wrong. Right Livelihood means you should earn your money in a way that's honest and which doesn't harm other people or cause problems in society. My mother never wanted to own a lot of luxury things anyway, so she wasn't greedy for money. She was happy with whatever was really necessary in her life and which she was able to afford. I'm glad she taught me to be the same way because it was good training for me when I later became a novice.

Like most of the other village children, I studied for my primary certificate at the local school. Few of us went on to study at the high school in the town. Most of the families were too poor to pay for bus fares and uniforms but anyway most parents, including my father, thought that high school education was a waste of time and money. They thought that after finishing primary school, the children should work in the rice paddies or the sugar cane fields. Only a few of the parents had gone to high school themselves and some hadn't even finished primary school, so they were almost illiterate. When I finished my primary certificate, I would have liked to go on to high school very much but even in the unlikely event of my father agreeing, it wouldn't have been possible. I accepted that there simply wasn't enough money, so I put the idea out of my mind. I already had enough beatings from my father without asking for more by being persistent about studying.

For several years after finishing primary school, I helped my mother on her food stall, took care of growing vegetables and helped around the house. Although I was happy being with my mother and helping her, the work soon became quite boring and seemed pointless. Even though it was honest work and just about brought in sufficient money, I couldn't imagine doing it for the rest of my life. I thought I could have a better future and the only way to achieve that was to become a novice and study. Always at the back of my mind was my dream of ordaining but as time went on, and the dream slipped further away, I started to get the idea that I just didn't know who I was, or what I was supposed to do with my life.

My father died from alcohol poisoning when he was about forty. I was sixteen then and after he died I was free to do what I most wanted. Although my father was often drunk and frequently hit my mother and me, I didn't hate him and I don't think he was an evil man in his heart. It was just the whisky that made him behave badly sometimes. If my father had been able to follow the precept about not drinking alcohol, I think we could have been a happier family. We would certainly have been less poor. When he wasn't drunk he could be quite kind and I'm sure he loved my mother and me. I say he wasn't a bad man because once he did a very compassionate thing, though I didn't know about it at the time. After my father died, my mother told me that she and my father had been divorced some years before. My father wanted it kept secret from me and they continued to live together, just so I would feel I was part of a family. I think that was a very kind thing to do. It made me sad that someone who was capable of such a caring thought should have wasted so much of his life and caused so much unhappiness to others, just because of his addiction to alcohol.

After my father died, my mother encouraged me to ordain immediately. I was very happy to realise my dream at last. I became a novice at our village monastery, where there were thirteen monks and one other novice. The novice was already my friend and he was a good boy. Like my mother, his parents had encouraged him to be a novice so he wouldn't be tempted into the same bad ways that other boys in our village followed.

Because I was always sure that I would become a monk when I was old enough, I decided that I should get my high school diploma and study even further if I had the opportunity. I thought monks should know as much as possible because it's their job to help teach and guide people. To do that, they have to understand not only Dhamma but many other things too. Although I believe they were all good men, most of the monks at my village monastery were not very well educated. Some of the older monks tried to teach Dhamma to the younger ones, but they never taught in a formal way and they weren't trained as teachers anyway. I realise now that sometimes their teaching wasn't even correct and was more about superstition and spirit worship, rather than real Dhamma. I decided I should move to another monastery with a high school as well as a proper religious school.

One of the old monks came from Nakhon Sawan and he told me that the province had several monasteries with good schools. Nakhon Sawan was about two hundred kilometres from my home and I wasn't sure if I wanted to move so far away, because I knew I would miss my mother. I talked it over with her. My mother said she would miss me too, but she wanted me to study. I stayed at my village monastery for about three months, until I knew the basics of living as a novice, and then made the move to Nakhon Sawan. Moving away from my village was a good thing, but leaving my mother behind was very hard for both of us. I can only go home once every few months and sometimes I get quite homesick. If I keep myself busy with my studies and duties, it's not so bad. My mother and I write to each other often and sometimes she sends me a little money, which I try to save for my next visit home.

I'm happy living at my monastery. There are about

fifty monks and twelve novices, so I have many friends. Although it is a large, busy and sometimes noisy monastery, it has its own mountain, so I can go up there when I want to meditate or just sit quietly on my own. Besides studying Pali and Dhamma and attending high school, I also have important duties at the monastery, so I am often very busy, especially early in the morning. What with my duties, my studies and my homework, my day lasts from 5am till about 11.30pm. Every morning after alms round and breakfast, I have to prepare the main temple hall for the morning service. I light the candles, set the incense sticks in their holder, arrange fresh flowers, sweep the marble steps and make sure everything is clean and tidy before the abbot arrives. Our hall is quite new and very beautiful, so I'm proud to have the duty to take care of it and I try to be conscientious. If I'm not, the abbot soon lets me know. Just before the service starts at 7.30am, I climb the tower and ring the big bell to let the monks know it's time for them to come to the hall.

Some novices are lazy about attending the morning service. Even when they do attend, they often fall asleep at the back of the hall. But I enjoy it and always attend because I like to pay my respects to the Buddha through the chanting. Our service isn't like worship in a Christian church. Most of the chants are the Buddha's teaching and some are the actual words of the Buddha, but we also chant the training rules of the monks and novices every day. I think it's good to start off the day with that reminder about how we should behave and I've learnt all seventy-five rules by heart. The abbot of the monastery seems to trust me, because besides allowing me to prepare the hall every day, he's also started giving me very young, temporary novices to take care of and train. I have to see that they're always dressed neatly in their robes, ensure they attend the services, give them small duties to do and take them on alms round with me. They usually stay at the monastery for about a month. They are usually only about eight or nine years old so they are quite a handful and can be very naughty sometimes, but I enjoy looking after them and teaching them how to behave. I feel quite proud when I walk on alms round with my own group of four or five little novices trotting along behind me, like a mother duck with her ducklings.

I study Pali and Dhamma at my own monastery every morning, but I study high school subjects in the afternoon at another monastery nearby. It's sometimes hard work studying at two schools at the same time and I think I get too much homework, but it's for my own benefit so I'm happy to do it. Although I'm not greedy for material things, I wish I had a computer, or even a typewriter, to use for my homework. My handwriting isn't very beautiful and I think it may be difficult for my teachers to read my reports sometimes, so maybe I get lower marks than some of the other students who can afford to type their reports at a computer shop. Despite my poor handwriting, my grades are quite good. I've already gained three certificates for Dhamma study, but I haven't got one for Pali yet. Pali is difficult but I persevere because I know it will be very helpful to me when I become a monk, because I'll be able to read the Buddhist scriptures in their original language. I'm also studying English, Mathematics, Thai, Science and Art at high school.

There are novices from several local monasteries studying at the high school. Some don't seem to make much effort to follow their precepts or rules and behave quite badly, so I try to avoid them. I understand why they may have difficulty. They are only young boys and some of them come from very poor backgrounds, or don't have much sense of discipline yet. The boys I'm most friendly with are those who are serious about being novices and who want to become monks when they are old enough. We understand that the ten novice precepts are very important, otherwise the Buddha wouldn't have given them to us.

Each precept has a definite and useful purpose. They help us to be kind to other people and all living creatures, to avoid bad things like telling lies, stealing and taking alcohol or drugs, to develop self-discipline and restraint, to avoid unnecessary luxury and to live our lives in a blameless way. That's all essential behaviour for a proper novice. Following the precepts also gives us confidence, because we know our behaviour can't be condemned or criticised by others. The biggest problem for some of the young novices seems to be the precept about not eating in the evening. Some of them think the precept isn't necessary and they eat whenever they want to, but I think it is important. We can eat as much as we want at lunchtime, so we shouldn't really need to eat in the evening. I get hungry sometimes, but I believe keeping the precept helps me become strong in my mind and helps me to overcome the physical feelings in my body. That strength and self-discipline helps me follow the other precepts as well. I've never yet eaten in the evening, though I have to admit I've sometimes been very tempted to.

I expect some of the novices have problems keeping other precepts too, especially about sexual things, but I believe a novice must try to keep himself pure. I know most boys do that sort of thing, but I think we have to remember that we're not ordinary boys; we are novice monks following the religious life. I try not to even think about girls because the Buddha taught us that all action is preceded by thought, so thinking about girls might lead me to break the precept. I would be very ashamed of myself if I did that, because I would think

156

I had failed the Buddha. I look at it like this: as a novice I have ten precepts. If I follow them strictly, I will be a novice one hundred per cent. If I break one precept, I will be a novice only ninety per cent. If I break two precepts, I will be a novice only eighty per cent and so on. I'm determined to be a novice one hundred per cent, so I mustn't break any of the precepts.

I don't find any of the precepts difficult to follow, because they clearly define for me who and what I am, and what is suitable behaviour for me as a novice and what isn't. Sometimes, though, precepts get broken without intention. For example, at my monastery we have a big fair at the end of the year to raise money for our building programme. The fair lasts three nights and there's usually a performance of Thai drama, a noisy music band, a movie, and Thai classical dancing with beautiful girls. Because all the monks and novices have to help at the fair, it's impossible not to see or hear the entertainment. Really, that breaks one of the novice precepts, but I can't do anything about it. Also, I have to go to my high school to study, so I have to pay my bus fare. That means handling money, so I break that precept nearly every day. I think the main thing is, though, that I don't want to break the precept, so that makes it not so bad. The Buddha taught us that our mental intention, good or bad, is the most important thing when we do anything. If I could live my life as a novice without breaking the precepts at all, even unintentionally, I would.

Although I know some novices have a problem with the precepts, their behaviour doesn't concern me too much. They have to practise as best they can, but I do get concerned when I see monks intentionally breaking their precepts. Then I feel I can't respect them any more, although their behaviour doesn't influence me to be less strict in my own practice as a novice. I get especially disappointed if there's a well-known monk that I believed practised well and whom I respected and admired, but who is discovered breaking his precepts and has to disrobe. Then I feel very let down by him. That's happened to several famous monks in Thailand in the last few years and I'm sorry about that. I'm sure it must be even more disappointing to the lay-people who followed the monk and believed him to be good. When I see a monk practising well, I am inspired to be the same.

Following the rules and precepts is only part of the novices' practice. We should also meditate and try to improve ourselves in every way we can. I don't think meditation is too difficult, although I don't seem to have much time to do it. I usually try to meditate for at least a few minutes before I go to bed, but on Wan Phra days, when both my schools are closed, I sometimes go up the mountain and sit there quietly for half an hour or so. The air is fresh at the top of the mountain and there's usually a cool breeze. I sit with my legs in the lotus position, with my hands in my lap, and breathe slowly in and out. It can make me feel very calm and helps reinforce the commitment in my mind to my life as a novice.

There are many different subjects for meditation and I haven't really studied it properly yet, but we can also use it to try to develop good qualities in the mind. That's what I try to do. The Buddha taught that there are four special qualities we should try to develop. One of them is to have a feeling of love and kindness towards other people and to hope they will be happy and free from suffering, just as we want to be ourselves. If more people had love and compassion for others, there would be fewer problems in the world, especially between people of different colours or religions, or from different cultural backgrounds. Another important quality we can develop is an understanding of the problems that all people share in common and to try to help others when we can. We should also try to have happy feelings when other people have success or good luck, instead of being envious of them. If we carry envy around in our minds, it can only have a bad effect on us and on everything we say or do. Finally, we should try to have a calm mind all the time, so we don't get angry or annoyed easily and can handle any problems that arise without making them more complicated or more difficult. All these special qualities can make us much better and nicer people, so they are not just helpful for monks and novices, or even just for Buddhists, but for everybody.

I wish Thai people would follow their five precepts more strictly and understand Dhamma more deeply. They should realise that the Dhamma is useful in every aspect of our lives, whoever we are and whatever work we do. The Buddha taught everybody how they could be good members of the community and contribute to society, the things to avoid, how to be generous and use wealth wisely, and how to develop good qualities. The Buddha even laid down special rules for kings and our King in Thailand follows the Buddha's teaching very strictly. He was even a monk for a time. But some people don't want to listen to the Buddha and are too caught up with their materialistic and selfish lifestyles. The monks and novices can help them by being good examples. Through their practice of going without luxury things, the monks can teach the people to be less greedy or not to think only of taking, and instead to think of giving more and having compassion for others. Greediness for material things seems to be a big problem now for many people in Thai society, especially young people. The monks can also help the people understand that they will inevitably be separated from all the things and the people they love, so they should never hold on too tightly to those things. If you hold on to anything too tightly, you will always suffer. People should respect the Buddha and follow his teaching and know that is the only way to be truly content. I think that probably describes me – truly content in my life as a novice monk.

9

Novice Wanchai

Cabbages and Dhamma

I come from a village in the north, close to the border with Laos. My province is called Nan. The province is so far north that most older people don't use Thai for everyday communication; they speak an ancient northern language called *Kammuang*. I grew up speaking Kammuang and didn't learn Thai properly until I went to primary school. Many years ago, Nan and the surrounding region had its own kings and was part of the Lanna Empire. My father told me that when my grandfather was born, Nan was still partly independent from the rest of Thailand, until the last Nan prince died in 1931. Many of the old people in my village still think that our region and province are different from the rest of the country and they're very proud of our history. Nan is a beautiful province, I think one of the most beautiful in Thailand, but I live more than six hundred kilometres away now and I haven't been home for a long time.

There's a saying in Thai that 'many children keep you poor'. I don't think my parents had heard that one, because they had nine children. I was the third and I'm now eighteen. I have six brothers and two sisters. The oldest is twenty-six and the youngest is only two. Poor rural people often have big families because farming in Thailand still relies greatly on manpower, rather than mechanical methods. If there are many children, even the young ones can work in the fields, or an older child can take care of the youngest at home, leaving the mother free to work. If the family doesn't have a lot of land, the children can go to the cities to get jobs and send money home to help support the family, especially when the parents are too old to work.

I think I have good parents. They were very loving and patient with all their children and seldom got angry with us. The only reason my mother would ever hit me was if I had a fight with one of my brothers, though I had so many brothers that happened nearly every day. I know my mother didn't really mean to hurt me, but she had a hard life. She was always tired from working in the fields from very early morning until late evening, then cooking and taking care of the children when she came home, so sometimes she became impatient if we were naughty or noisy. I think she was a good mother to us and we were a happy family.

My parents didn't have any land of their own, but they rented a few acres from a neighbour. Even though we were a large family and didn't own any land, I don't think we were particularly poor when I was younger, or at least not by the normal standards of rural people. We were fairly self-sufficient and a lot of the food we grew was for ourselves. Whatever we didn't need was sold. My parents earned about 15,000 baht a year from the crop, so they didn't have much spare money but we always had enough food, even if it was only rice and cabbages. We got good harvests in Nan and there were always plenty of cabbages. Even in those days, just a few years ago, I don't think country people judged their poverty or wealth only by counting their money or by the things they owned. If the family had enough food and somewhere to live, and if the rice was growing, that was sufficient to make people content. I don't think anybody really expected much more and the idea of becoming wealthy and owning a lot of material things didn't enter their heads. I think that attitude has changed now and people want more than just what is essential or necessary in their lives. I suppose it's human nature to want more things, but it's stupid to think they will make you more content. Often, I think owning lots of things just makes life more complicated and only leads to wanting more and more.

My village was quite large, with about two hundred old wooden houses and nearly a thousand people. There was a wide river near to the village, so my friends and I were able to fish for food and go swimming. In the rainy season, the river always overflowed and usually covered the wooden bridge. The track to the village ended at the bridge, so when the river was flooded we were completely cut off from everywhere. That was good as far as my friends and I were concerned because it meant we couldn't cross the bridge to go to primary school for a couple of months, until the water had subsided. The village itself was on a hill, so it was never flooded.

I studied at primary school for only two years. When I was eight, I had to leave school so I could take my turn in looking after my younger brothers and sister, which was a full-time job. For large families in rural areas, the children's education usually has to take second place to the financial and overall needs of the family, so it didn't bother me to leave school early. I'd never expected to be able to study beyond the second or third year of primary school, so I wasn't disappointed at all. I never enjoyed studying much when I was very young anyway. It seemed pointless for someone in my situation.

I don't know if many children keep you poor, but I do know that having to take care of lots of younger brothers all day can drive you crazy. I didn't mind looking after the little ones at first. There weren't so many of them then, but there always seemed to be another one on the way. One time, my mother had twins, which was a shock for all of us and gave me a lot of extra work. The babies were always crying or making a fuss and I would have preferred working on the farm. I loved them all, but they drove me mad sometimes. I was the baby-minder for several years, from when I was eight until I was about eleven, then my younger brother was old enough to take over the job and I went to work in the fields.

Like all the families in the village, we grew rice, ginger and cabbages. I would have liked to work in the rice fields but I got the job of taking care of the cabbages. That wasn't much fun, but baby cabbages are a lot better behaved than baby boys and don't cause nearly as many problems. Now, I'm glad there are a lot of children in the family because it's good to have so many brothers and sisters, but if I get married I don't think I'd like such a large family of my own.

Even though I only studied at primary school for two years, I was happy with that and there didn't seem any reason to study further. I'd learned to count and read and I thought that was about all I needed from school. The babies and cabbages needed to be counted sometimes, but even learning to read didn't really seem essential. We never saw newspapers or magazines in the village and, in my house at least, we didn't have a single book. Nobody had time to read anyway because there was always work to be done. Learning about Mathematics, Science, History, English or Art seemed a waste of time for people in our situation, who usually started working at age eight or nine and carried on working every day until they dropped dead. If I was going to grow rice and cabbages for the rest of my life, which is what I thought I would be doing, what use was education to me? Why should I need to know about English grammar, or who Leonardo Da Vinci was? I realise now that was a very narrow view, but poor rural people don't have much opportunity to broaden their views. They start off ignorant and usually remain that way. Maybe the idea of growing cabbages doesn't sound like a very exciting prospect, but I didn't know and couldn't imagine any other way of life at that time. I was content to do what my family had done for generations. I never questioned my life or thought about the future. My thoughts hardly went further than the boundaries of the village. I've broadened my ideas a lot since then, though I'm still not sure about my future. Looking after about a thousand cabbages from dawn till dusk was boring, but I didn't mind my work and had no need to think about alternatives. Neither was there any reason for me to think about becoming a novice. I'd only been in the nearby monastery a couple of times and I wasn't interested in religion at all.

Although my parents said they were Buddhist, I don't think either of them knew much about Dhamma and my father had never been a novice or monk. Although it's traditional that Thai men ordain before they get married, my father married when he was quite young and babies started coming non-stop after that, so he never had the opportunity. Like most Thai people, my parents liked to hear the traditional stories about the Buddha's previous lives, but that was about all. They were more concerned about whether there would be drought or flood, the state of the crops, or the selling price of rice and cabbages. My father and mother are good people, but they were poorly educated and neither studied beyond primary school. Like most of the other villagers, they were very superstitious and frightened of ghosts. They often talked about the spirits of the land and ways to keep them happy so we could have a good harvest. Outside our house was a little shrine for the spirits, and my mother offered rice and water there every morning. I'm the only person in my family who has ever been a novice or studied Dhamma, so I have different ideas to my parents now. When I'm able to visit home, I try to explain Dhamma to them. They understand it, but they still cling to their old beliefs just as strongly because those beliefs seem more relevant to their daily lives.

I'm not sure what happened, but there came a time when my family did become quite poor. I think there had been a drought that year and my parents started to get into debt. Even my father's motorcycle was taken away by the finance company. We either needed more money coming in, or less going out. My father thought I was too young to go Bangkok to work, so he suggested I should ordain as a novice, to help relieve the financial burden on the family. I was very unhappy about the idea. I knew that if I were a novice I would miss out on all the things that my friends and I liked to do and I wouldn't have any fun any more. I think the best time for having fun is when you're young, especially for children from farming families. After that, we only have endless hard work to look forward to for the rest of our lives, plus all the problems of bringing up a family. For children from poor families, childhood is a very short period and I didn't want to waste mine by being stuck in a dull monastery. Despite my feelings, it was obvious that someone had to leave the home and I was the only son of about the right age to ordain. Even if I couldn't contribute to the family income, I could at least help ease the financial problem. I think my father realised I wasn't very happy. He told me that if I really disliked the novice life, I could disrobe and return home and the next son could ordain instead. Knowing I had his permission to disrobe made me happier, but I still didn't really want to do it, despite my younger brother's sudden and desperate encouragement.

Although my father wanted me to ordain because of our financial problems, he suggested I should use the opportunity to study. I think he was just trying to make the idea of ordaining sound more interesting to me – which it didn't – but I agreed anyway. Our village monastery was very small and didn't offer any tuition in anything, so my father decided I should ordain at another monastery which had a school, even though it was quite far away. I was very miserable about that because I loved all my family very much and I didn't like the idea of not seeing my brothers and sisters so often. In a way then, I felt my father was rejecting me by sending me so far away, but I had no choice and had to accept his decision. I ordained when I was thirteen at a monastery about fifty kilometres from my village. Looking back, I realise that was a good thing. If I'd ordained in the village monastery and was able to visit my family often, I might not have settled into the novice life so easily, nor progressed in my studies. I think I might have turned into a lazy novice, which would have made ordaining pointless.

I don't think my father realised that the monastery he sent me to live at taught only religious subjects. I decided that if I had to be a novice, I should make the best of it by finishing my primary education. That seemed more immediately useful than studying Pali and Dhamma, neither of which interested me at all then. After about a month, I decided to move and went to live at another monastery that had a primary school. The school wasn't really very good but the primary course was short and I had my certificate within about two years. I was pleased with that small achievement and it gave me the incentive to want to carry on studying for my high school certificate and diploma.

To continue my studies meant moving again. By that time, I'd got used to not seeing my family and I had become more independent. I decided I might just as well move a long way and live in a completely different province, so I could see something of my own country. Even so, I think I was quite adventurous in moving six hundred kilometres to my present monastery in Nakhon Sawan. The idea of studying was gradually building up in my mind and I'd become more interested in Pali and Dhamma by then. I'd heard the monastery in Nakhon Sawan was near to a special high school and had its own religious school, so I thought it might suit me.

Although the monastery school teaches only religious subjects, novices can also study at a special government high school nearby. I was quite surprised at how much I enjoyed studying. By the time I finished third grade of high school, I'd become interested in trying to get a diploma for Pali studies too. All the novices at the monastery school enjoy studying Dhamma but most of them dislike Pali because the grammar is so difficult. I didn't like it at first either, but it became a sort of challenge to me.

It's really only the opportunity to study and the challenge of Pali that stops me from disrobing, though I have no clear idea yet of what I would do if I wasn't a novice. I may disrobe when I reach twenty anyway, but I won't decide about that until I pass the third grade of Pali. There are nine grades. The first two are relatively easy and I've passed them, but the third level is much harder and can take years to pass. I failed that exam last year. If I'd passed, I would have had the title *Maha*, which means 'great', and I would have been called Novice Maha Wanchai. Many monks have the title, but it's more unusual for a novice and I want to be a Maha very much. It's not exactly of any use, but lay-people have a lot of respect for monks or novices with the title and I think it would make my parents very proud of me. It would make me proud of myself too because it would be quite an achievement. I studied hard for the exam and when I failed I was so depressed I considered disrobing and returning home immediately. When I thought about it a bit more carefully, and pictured endless rows of cabbages and babies stretching into the future, I changed my mind and decided to carry on studying until I pass the exam. At least then I will have something to show for my time as a novice, even if I disrobe afterwards, and it will also give me more time to think about my future.

I think studying and living away from my village has really opened my mind and made me think much more about the possibilities for my future. I've no clear idea yet of what I would eventually like to do, but I'm taking one step at a time and not planning too far ahead. Maybe that doesn't sound very positive, but at least now I can see alternative possibilities, other than just following in my father's footsteps, as I expected to do a few years ago. At the moment, I want my Pali certificate and my sixth grade high school diploma. I'm not sure beyond that, because the more I study the more my ideas change, but growing cabbages for the rest of my life is becoming the last option. My ideas are constantly changing now because I've suddenly become surrounded by books all day and for the first time I'm really enjoying reading.

At my monastery we have a new and very good library. It has hundreds of books about many subjects, not just religion, and the abbot has recently given me the job of librarian. Because my library duty prevents me from chanting at funerals, the abbot gives me 300 baht every month. That's the only money I have and my parents have never been able to send me any, but it's enough for me. I have to be in the library for about five hours a day, five days a week. Sometimes I grumble about that (to myself, not to the abbot), because I still have to go to school as well, so I don't have much time to spend with my novice friends, or for watching TV or playing football. We shouldn't play football anyway, so I suppose not having too much free time helps keeps me out of mischief. Although I sometimes complain, I know how lucky I am to be surrounded by so many books.

Not many monks or novices use the library, so after cleaning the floor each morning and dusting the shelves I don't have anything to do except read. Besides having plenty of time now to study Pali in the library, I've also become interested in many other things too, which I'd never even thought about before. I wasn't particularly interested in my studies when I was younger because then I thought I would be a cabbage farmer all my life. I'd never read any book except my primary school books and they always seemed boring. Being surrounded by so many different books and magazines and – more importantly – deciding for myself what I want to read, has really started to broaden my mind, even more so than studying at high school. Studying at school is really just about absorbing facts, but just flicking through magazines and newspapers and reading the occasional article has helped give me an understanding of how much is going on in the world, which I never even thought about when I lived in the village. I like reading computer magazines, science and natural history books, but most especially books about agriculture.

Reading about agriculture has made me understand that many of the farming methods used in my village are very old-fashioned and inefficient. I even once found an old magazine with an article about growing cabbages, which made me realise there are better ways of doing it than we followed on the family farm. Although most of the farmers in my village understand the land, they really don't seem to understand agriculture as a science at all. They just follow the same ways that have been used for generations and pass on those ways to their children, so there's never much real progress. Many don't even use modern chemical fertilisers, though that's mainly because they can't afford them. It's probably a good thing to keep to some traditional methods, but I can see quite a few ways for them to improve and get better yields from their land. All the farmers grow rice, ginger and cabbages because that's what their families have done for hundreds of years. But I'm sure the soil and climate in our region is good enough to grow crops that would give a better financial return, or which are at less risk from fluctuating market prices. Anybody can grow a cabbage.

As most of the families have many children and plenty of available labour, few farmers bother with tractors or modern harvesters, relying instead on manpower or buffaloes. Probably most couldn't afford tractors anyway, but for some they could be a good investment. I don't really want to physically work on the land but if I had the opportunity I think I'd like to study agriculture as a science and try to help the people in my village to improve their lives. The government has a lot of colleges in Thailand where poor students from farming families can study basic agriculture, fisheries and animal husbandry without having to pay fees, if they first have a third grade high school certificate. The students get free accommodation on campus and free food during the two years' course. That might be one possibility for me if I disrobe because my parents wouldn't need to support me or pay college fees. Some students who finish their course at the colleges are able to get university scholarships to study for degrees in agricultural science, which is another possibility worth thinking about for the future. I think everybody in my village would die of shock if I went home with a university degree.

For the present, I'm not unhappy as a novice because I know it's the only way I can study, but there are a few things I regret I can't do. The last time I went home, which was for the Thai New Year festival about two years ago, I was quite upset that I couldn't take part in the family activities. All my brothers and sisters were at home for the festival but I felt left out of everything. Even at home I had to behave as a novice, because that's what everybody expected of me, so I couldn't share my meals with the family and I had to eat alone. I couldn't help in the fields, or go fishing or swimming, or do any of the things that ordinary boys do. My brothers played football and I wanted to join in, but I had to watch from the sidelines. I couldn't even cheer when a goal was scored because novices aren't allowed to be noisy. It would have shocked some of the villagers if they had seen me doing those things. They might have thought I was a bad novice and my parents would have been ashamed of me. I want my parents to be proud of me, so I behaved as best I could all the time. Some of my brothers have got girlfriends in the village now and they told me what a good feeling it is to have a girlfriend. That made me quite envious of them. I'm eighteen now and I think about those things sometimes, but I know I just have to make the best I can of my life and not worry too much about what I can't do.

Although being a novice prevents me from doing some things I would like to do, the precepts also prevent me from doing bad things, like drinking alcohol or taking drugs. Everybody has that precept and I think it's the most important. If people get drunk or take drugs, they can't think clearly and that can lead to breaking other precepts, like killing or stealing, and maybe getting into a lot of trouble. As a novice, I feel I'm protected from the temptation to drink or take drugs, but learning Dhamma has made me not want them anyway. I feel sorry for young people who are addicted to dangerous drugs. They must know drugs are not a good thing, but I think they are influenced by their friends, or maybe their parents don't take proper care of them. Perhaps they see their lives in the villages as being at a dead end, even when they're young. I'm sure if they understood Dhamma better they wouldn't need to take drugs. When I last went home, I gave my little brothers a Dhamma lecture about the dangers of drugs and alcohol. I don't think they're involved with those things but I'll do my best to make sure they don't get tempted. I think my little brothers have a lot of respect for me because I am a novice, so they listen to me when I try to guide them.

I think some other novice precepts are not so beneficial

or important, like not eating in the evening. I don't eat every evening, but if I feel hungry I eat and I don't really feel guilty about it. I wouldn't let anybody see me eating, so perhaps I do feel a little guilty inside, or maybe I just don't want people to think I'm a bad novice. Always telling the truth can be difficult too. When I last went home, I had to have my abbot's permission. He asked me how long I would be away and I said three days, though I knew it would be a week. But if I'd told him I would be away for a week, he wouldn't have let me go, so I had to tell a lie. It was only a small lie, but I'm sorry about it because telling any lie, especially to the abbot, is wicked.

I try my best to follow all the precepts because I know they are important to us, otherwise we would be just the same as ordinary boys instead of novice monks. I'd like to be an ordinary boy sometimes, but I'm not, so I have a duty to follow the novice precepts and I accept that. I'm not very successful sometimes at keeping all the precepts, but I guess I'm an average novice; better than some and worse than others. On the whole, living as a novice has been very good for me, particularly because it's given me the opportunity to broaden my mind about so many things, which certainly wouldn't have happened if I'd stayed in the village. I'd like to suggest to my little brother that he should ordain too, if my father can spare him from the farm. I'm sure he'll hate the idea as much as I did at first, but I'd like to see him have the opportunity for an education too.

Although I may not be a particularly good novice, I admire monks and novices who do practise well. I especially admire Phra Ajahn Buddhadasa, who lived in the south of Thailand at a monastery called Wat Suan Mokh. He died more than ten years ago, but he was famous all over Thailand and people will always remember him. Ajahn Buddhadasa only had the same education as me, to third grade of high school and basic Pali studies, but he was given five honorary doctorates because of his deep understanding of Buddhism. That's quite inspiring to me and shows that understanding is quite different and more important than just learning. The Ajahn cared very much about Thai people and our society and culture. He could see how Thai society was being affected by materialism, greed and by bad influences from other countries. He could sometimes be very direct and down to earth in his style of teaching but his words really make people stop and think about their lives. I'd never heard of Ajahn Buddhadasa until I started working in the monastery library. He wrote many books; I've read all of them and they have had a good effect on me.

Although the Ajahn doesn't necessarily inspire me to want to devote my life to being a monk, he does inspire me to want to be a good person and to follow the

Dhamma all my life. Because I've had the good opportunity to live as a novice, I know that the Dhamma is always there to protect me and support me, whatever situation I find myself in, or whatever problems I have to face. I understand how all of us can use it in our lives, even if we are only cabbage farmers. Understanding just that was worth becoming a novice for.

10

Novice Maha Sorasing

Breaking free

I f I had to choose one word to try to sum up my early childhood, I would choose *determination*. Not my own – that developed later – but rather my mother's determination that I should have the opportunity to make something of my life. Without her determination and the sacrifices she was prepared to make for me, I'd probably have achieved nothing at all. Instead, I would have remained trapped in a generations-old cycle of poverty and despair, with no escape. Eventually, I would probably have passed on that same poverty and despair to my own children.

I'm an only child and was born in what was really just a hovel in a village in the north of Thailand. When my parents were married they had no money and nowhere to live, so they simply looked for the nearest deserted shack and moved into it. In my village, if a building had a couple of walls standing and something on top to keep the rain out, it could be called home. Our shack had no electricity, no toilet or washroom and no running water. From as soon as I was strong enough to carry a bucket, it became my job to fetch water from a tap, which was a considerable distance away. We were almost destitute, but there was no shame in our poverty; it was just the way things were. There were plenty of families in the village even worse off than we were. Almost the entire community was poor and the only people who had any money at all were the drug dealers. The village was in Uttaradit Province and close to the border with Laos, so it was convenient for the dealers, who mostly sold heroin and amphetamines. Some of my village friends were taking one or the other by the time they left primary school.

My particular village was tiny, with only about 500 people, but several nearby villages had grown and almost absorbed it, until we had become like the poor suburb of a small town. There were probably about 2,000 houses and 5,000 people in the immediate area. Although there were a lot of people in the group of villages, the majority of the villagers in our part were either old people or children of primary school age. There were few teenagers. Some were able to study at high school but most went off to Bangkok or the other big cities as soon as they finished their primary education. Few had any choice in the matter and some left the village even before they finished primary school. Because they weren't well educated, or even literate in some cases, they worked as labourers on building sites, or as maids, gardeners and in other menial jobs. Northern people are often physically very attractive and have paler skins than many Thais so some – boys as well as girls – ended up working in places like Pattaya, where they could always find work in the sex clubs and go-go bars.

I don't think they did that sort of work because they enjoyed it, but to young people without any educational qualifications, working in the 'entertainment industry' probably seemed like an easy way to make money; much more money than could ever be gained from less unwholesome employment. The long-term health risks and moral issues had to be laid aside or forgotten, simply because the daily need to survive and help support the family was more immediately important. Whatever work the young people did, they only rarely came back to the village, although most regularly sent money home to their parents, which was the only way the old people could manage. It was a rice-farming region but most of the villagers in our part of town had little land and grew only what they needed for their daily needs, relying instead on the money sent home by their children.

My father had only a tiny area of borrowed land on which he grew a small crop of green onions. My mother sold the onions, but mostly we had to manage on whatever money my father could earn from doing odd jobs in the neighbours' rice paddies. Most of the neighbours were almost as poor as we were, so my father earned very little; usually less than twenty baht a day but often nothing at all if there was no work to be done. Ours was always a hand-to-mouth existence and every new day brought the same problem of simply finding food to eat. We ate whatever my mother could find growing or crawling about in the fields, with onions. Usually, the only meat we had came from rats, which my father caught in the rice paddies. A lot of poor, rural Thai people eat rats, but only those caught in the fields. House rats are considered dirty and inedible. Although we often had little food and I was a skinny and sickly boy, my mother was a big woman, but that was the result of some long-term illness which made her very overweight. My father was a small man, so in my parents' frequent fights it was usually him that came off worst.

My parents argued almost constantly, and because of

this, I understood from a very young age that they didn't like being together. I suppose they must have loved each other once but they had difficulty living together because our extreme poverty caused such a continuous strain on their relationship. Our poverty was always there, always at the root of my parents' problems. They had terrible arguments, when each blamed the other for the desperate situation we were in.

Even as a very young boy and without any real under-standing of what the arguments were about, I always silently sided with my mother. Perhaps that was unfair to my father, but I adored my mother. To me, she could do no wrong. In a way, I think my mother relied on me almost as much as I did on her. I believe my needs drove her on and gave her a reason for continuing to struggle with our desperate situation. Without me to fight for, she might just have given up, as my father seemed to have done. She was devoted to me and desper-ately wanted me to make something of my life; to break out of the cycle of poverty she felt we were trapped in. She sometimes said that poverty was like an inherited disease. She said that she had got it from her parents but that she had no intention of passing it on to me, or to my children. I believe my mother eventually sacri-ficed her own life for me, determined to give me the opportunity to break free of our poverty. I think she was frightened that I would inevitably end up like some of the other youngsters in the village or worse, from her point of view, like my father.

I don't know why, but some Thai people seem to assume that poor people are automatically bad people. They look down on them just because of their poverty or lack of education. Poor or not, I believe my mother was a very good woman. She hadn't had any education at all, but even when I was very young she taught me Dhamma. I don't think she knew she was teaching Dhamma because she didn't particularly relate it to Buddhism; she just tried to explain what she believed was the right way for me to live my life. I doubt if my mother had ever learned the five precepts for lay-people but she didn't need to – they were already in her heart. It was only much later, after I became a novice, that I realised her teaching was the same as the Buddha's in many respects. My mother was a naturally good woman with a natural sense of Dhamma.

I'm not at all sure how I felt about my father when I was very young. I must have loved him then, as all children do, but my feelings never really had the chance to develop or mature, because of what happened later. I suppose I didn't know my father very well and, by the time I did, it was too late. Any loving feelings I had for him and which might have grown as I got older, disappeared when he walked out on us when I was nine. I'm sorry to say that I later came to despise him, at least for a time. It wouldn't be fair to call my father a bad man, though he was certainly a lazy and apathetic one. He didn't drink a lot or take drugs – he had no money for either anyway – and he never beat me. That wasn't because I was such a good little boy, but rather because he simply couldn't be bothered to beat me, though I'm sure my mother wouldn't have let him, even if I'd deserved it. My father probably thought he tried his best for us, but when you start off with absolutely nothing, it must be difficult to progress to anything better and it becomes easy to slip into apathy. Both he and my mother had come from families that were as destitute as we were. They were both either orphaned or abandoned early in their lives, they weren't educated and they had no land, so that wasn't a good start for them and they could find no way to even begin to escape from their situation.

I think because of his own upbringing, my father didn't really expect much from life and he wasn't too bothered about the way we were forced to live, or certainly not as much as my mother. My father had no dreams or ambition for himself, or for us. Maybe from my mother's point of view he didn't try hard enough, especially in helping me to progress. My father was interested only in our day-to-day survival, because he had to be, but my mother looked more to the future, and especially my future.

Despite coming from a very poor and unhappy background, that didn't make me an unhappy child, though I was frequently a hungry one. In fact, I was very happy and carefree right up to the time my father left. I played constantly with my friends, getting up to all the usual mischief which little boys love. We were lucky because we had so much to occupy our time. Our village was in a beautiful environment, surrounded by mountains, forests and a river, so we were never bored.

I attended a local primary school. I'd been excited about the prospect for months and I loved studying from the very first day. Every subject was of interest and the school day seemed too short to me. I particularly enjoyed studying Thai. That was a great challenge because until then I'd usually spoken Kammuang, the northern language used in the region. I practically gave up playing with my friends because I just wanted to read and reread my schoolbooks every evening and practise writing in Thai script. I would read until it was too dark to see by candlelight, and excitedly share every new fact I learned with my mother. My grades were good in every subject and my mother was very proud of me, encouraging me as much as she could. Even then, I thought there could be nothing better than to be a teacher and go to school every day. That dream, as silly and unattainable as it seemed at the time, never left me.

A couple of years before I finished primary school, my parents had one of their big fights. It was the biggest they'd ever had, though it was to be the last. Although I was only eight or nine, my father said that I had to leave school and either get work locally or go to Bangkok to find a job, which some of my friends had already done. What I wanted was of no importance, but I understood that. We were desperate for money and to my father the only solution – the traditional solution for people like us – was for me to work, whatever work I did, and even though I was so young. My mother not only refused to allow me to leave primary school, she insisted that my father find some way to send me to high school too. He laughed and said that was impossible. To him, it really was impossible. My mother argued that I had to carry on studying because it was the only way I would ever have the chance to achieve anything at all, or to break away from the poverty that she and my father had inflicted on me. She knew how much I wanted to study and I think she was frightened that I would turn into a replica of my father; uneducated, struggling from day to day, living from hand to mouth. I think she was also terrified of the idea of me going to the big city alone, having seen what had happened to some of the other youngsters in the village. She said that if anybody went to Bangkok, it should be my father. That was really the sensible option in the situation. He refused, I think just because he was so apathetic.

The argument dragged on for months. The bad feeling between my parents got worse and worse until one day my father simply walked out. He left without even saying goodbye to us. Apparently, he did go to Bangkok and got a labouring job, but we never heard from him and he never sent a single baht home to help my mother and me. My mother was very angry and disappointed by my father's desertion – of me, not of her – but if anything it made her even more determined to find some way for me to continue studying beyond primary school.

When my father left us, my childhood came to a very sudden end. We had absolutely no income at all, except for the few baht my mother earned by selling onions. I'd just turned ten years old, but it fell to me to find whatever work I could in the village to try and support my mother and myself. My mother's illness was becoming worse and she often felt unwell, though she never let that stop her doing whatever needed to be done. Despite being a big woman and mentally very strong, she was physically quite weak. Although I still went to primary school every day, I also took over my father's odd jobs in the neighbours' fields in the early morning and late evening or, when I wasn't needed there, walked from house to house asking if anybody wanted any help. I suppose I became little more than a beggar but if I earned or was given just a few baht I thought I was lucky; it meant my mother and I could survive another day. I was terribly unhappy with my life but I had no options and I felt a very strong sense of duty to my mother.

Throughout the next year or so, until I finished my primary studies, I was constantly lethargic from lack of sleep and insufficient food. On a couple of occasions, dealers offered me free amphetamines to give me more energy. That's just a way of getting people addicted, so they have to buy pills in future. I always refused, though sometimes I was so desperate I considered risking my mother's anger and accepting. I'm glad I never did, but often I was so tired I could hardly drag myself to school. Sometimes I even fell asleep at my desk but I never missed a single lesson, though my grades dropped badly. Despite my constant exhaustion, I was determined not to give up my primary studies because it seemed increasingly unlikely that I would ever be able to study beyond that. Although my mother was determined that I should study at high school, I knew there was no possibility of it. She couldn't afford to buy a pencil for me, let alone school shoes. My mother's brother lived nearby and she even begged for his help to send me to high school, but my uncle had a large family of his own and was as destitute as we were. There was really nowhere for us to turn and the future looked very bleak.

On my last day of primary school, I was desperately depressed. With my study days over, I had to face my future and what I saw stretching ahead frightened me. We had no land for me to work on, the neighbours couldn't afford to employ me and there was almost nothing for me to do all day except scavenge for food. My mother blamed herself as much as my father for our situation and became increasingly anxious about my future; always *my* future, never her own. Our situation seemed hopeless and I began to think seriously of going to Bangkok to find work, so I could not only support my mother but also save money to enable me to study later. I think I would have been willing to do almost anything for the opportunity to study. I tried to discuss it with my mother and that was one of the few times she ever became angry with me. She refused to allow me to go to the city and insisted that she would work something out. We carried on for about another year, both of us sinking more and more into despair.

I had just turned twelve when my mother told me she had decided to go to Bangkok herself to get a job. A friend of hers from the village was working in a factory in the city and had written to say that some unskilled jobs were available. She even sent the bus fare to my mother. The job meant working long hours for little

money but my mother was sure that if she worked overtime as well, she could support herself and send enough
home to cover the cost of my uniform, books and bus
fares for at least the first few years of high school. She
tried to sound cheerful and enthusiastic about the plan,
but I knew she wasn't really because she disliked and
feared the city intensely. She had already spoken with
my uncle and he had reluctantly agreed to take me
in. My uncle was a good man but he lived in a tiny,
two-roomed shack with his wife and six children, as
well as a cousin or two. It was already overcrowded
but I suppose he felt that one more wouldn't make
much difference. I didn't like the idea of staying with
my uncle and his big family but I said nothing because
it hardly seemed important compared to the sacrifice
my mother was prepared to make for me.

I couldn't bear the idea of my mother working in
Bangkok and I begged her not to go. I told her that
her health wasn't good enough. I told her I didn't want
to go to high school. I told her I would go to Bangkok
instead. She wouldn't listen. She had made her decision and there was absolutely no way to change her
mind. Her health really wasn't good but she was determined that I would study, even if it meant we had to
be separated for long periods. Whichever one of us
went to Bangkok, separation was unavoidable, but she
said she would rather know that I was safe in the

village with my uncle than at risk in the city. I know she was frightened that if I went to the city, I would return as a drunk, a drug addict, or dying from AIDS. Her fears may have been justified because there were other young people in the village who had come home with the same problems. If my mother went to Bangkok, we knew we wouldn't see each other for a long time. The factory gave its workers only a few days off each year, and my mother wouldn't be able to return home for nearly nine months, until the next New Year holiday.

On the day my mother left, I didn't want to say goodbye by making her upset with my tears, but I had a struggle to hold them back. Saying goodbye to her was probably the hardest thing I'd ever done. I thought my heart would break. I think my mother felt the same way. She didn't even want me to go to the city bus station to see her off on her long journey, because she knew that would just prolong our sadness. Dry-eyed, we hugged each other for a long time and she promised me that everything would work out well. Then I watched her walk down the track towards the local bus stop, carrying a shoddy old bag with her few things in. I wanted to run after her and beg her not to go but I knew nothing could stop her. She paused at a corner and turned to look back. She smiled and waved to me and I felt such a surge of love that I could no longer hold back my tears. The moment she disappeared around the corner, I fell to my knees and sobbed like a baby. I never saw my mother again.

About six months later, my uncle received a letter from my mother's friend in Bangkok. The letter said that my mother had died from what may have been diabetes. She had been working every day and most of every night to try to save money for my education, even though she knew her illness was getting worse each day. Just before she died, my mother told her friend to let me know that she loved me very much and that she wanted me to ordain as a novice monk. She said that I should try my best to be a good novice and that I should study as much and as hard as I could. Even at her death, she was thinking only of my future. I was devastated by her death and for a time I blamed myself. I was sure that if my mother hadn't gone to work in Bangkok she wouldn't have died, and she had gone only because I wanted to study. My uncle and his family were very loving to me then and I don't know what might have happened to me without their kindness and support. My uncle was also very upset about his sister's death and blamed my father bitterly. Now, I think that was unfair but at the time I hated and despised my father.

My uncle agreed that becoming a novice was the right course for me. I know he would have helped me study at high school if he could but he didn't even have the money to educate his own children. Even if he hadn't agreed, I would still have ordained because that was what my mother wanted. Anyway, the only other options were that I should stay in the village doing odd jobs for the rest of my life, or go to Bangkok to labour on building sites for the rest of my life. If I stayed in the village, I would probably meet a girl, get married, raise our children in a hovel, give them rats to eat and force them to leave school at age ten to find work. My father's story repeated. If I went to Bangkok, I'd labour all day to earn a few baht which I'd likely spend on drink to help me forget the day, or on drugs to give me the energy to work the next day. Neither option was worth considering and neither was what my mother wanted. I would become a novice monk and I would study.

None of the little local monasteries offered any opportunities for study at all, so I ordained at a larger one nearer the provincial city. That monastery had only a junior high school but it did have quite a good Dhamma and basic Pali school. I was only twelve and I knew I would be a novice for many years, so I decided that I should first learn what that meant by trying to understand the Buddha's teaching as thoroughly as I could. I was determined to do my best as a novice, as much for my mother as for myself. I could never forget what I thought of as her great sacrifice for me. I've never forgotten it. It's always been there, driving me forward.

Almost as soon as I ordained, I became fascinated by Pali, even more so when I learned it was possible to earn the title Maha for passing the difficult third grade. Few young novices achieve that. It can take many years of study, but I was determined that I could do it, even though it meant studying night and day. That was the first challenge I'd ever really had, so maybe I wanted to prove something to myself. I passed the first grade in my second year as a novice, the second grade in my third year and then, to everybody's amazement, the third grade on my first attempt the following year. At sixteen, I became Novice Maha Sorasing. I was invited to go to Bangkok to receive my title and ceremonial fan from one of the most senior monks in Thailand. I was very proud that day, and I know my mother would have been proud of me too.

At my monastery, it wasn't possible to study beyond the third grade of Pali because there were no sufficiently qualified teachers there. I wanted to carry on studying Pali and Dhamma but I also needed to continue my high school studies, so I had to think about moving. Although it was two hundred kilometres away, I decided to transfer to a monastery in Nakhon Sawan Province that had a better religious school, as well as a good high school. Moving so far didn't bother me because I had no emotional ties or responsibilities. But just before I moved, I had a shock. My father turned up.

I don't know how my father knew I was a novice or that I was living at the monastery. He hadn't yet been back to the village, nor spoken with my uncle. He greeted me almost as though he'd never been away, then asked if my mother was well. All the bitterness I thought I'd overcome welled up in me for a moment, but quickly subsided again. I'd learnt a lot of Dhamma by then and that had given me a good understanding of life and helped my feelings mature, despite my young age. My father had become an alcoholic and he looked such a pathetic figure that I felt only compassion for him. I'd already realised that his own early years had been every bit as difficult as mine. He was caught in the same trap, had suffered from the same poverty, the same lack of opportunities and with probably much the same heart-breaks. I knew he couldn't really be blamed for the ways things had turned out for us. I told him gently that my mother was dead. He was quite obviously shocked and genuinely upset by the news. I didn't ask him any questions about his life in Bangkok, why he hadn't sent my mother any money or why he had returned after seven years; there didn't seem any point in recriminations. He left soon after. I've seen him only once since then, for a few minutes, when I returned to the village a year ago to visit my uncle. My father was living alone in the same hovel in which I was born, growing a few onions and doing odd jobs for the neighbours. He was just about surviving.

I made the move to Nakhon Sawan and I am very happy, though the practice for a novice in the lower northern region is sometimes different from my first monastery. In the far north, a couple of odd traditions have developed. In many monasteries there, it's quite acceptable for monks and novices to eat in the evening. They don't have to do it secretly, as some young novices do at my present monastery. Instead, lay-people come to offer dinner and the monks and novices eat quite openly. Also, monks and novices are allowed to wear ordinary underwear beneath their robes, which they don't in the lower north. Maybe that's something to do with the weather being cooler in the far north. I've no idea how those traditions developed, but it was a bit of a shock to find I couldn't eat in the evening after I moved.

As a novice, I keep all the precepts as well as I can. I value them because they've helped me become self-disciplined, independent, confident about my behaviour and very determined, though perhaps determination is something I inherited from my mother.

I'm eighteen now and will soon complete my high school studies. I've also passed the fourth grade in Pali, but I think that will be the highest I will go because I intend to disrobe as soon as I have my high school diploma. As my mother always knew, that diploma is the key that will set me free. I'm planning for the future now and I feel very confident. I've already been offered a scholarship to study for a Bachelor degree in Thai at a teacher-training institute, if I can pass the entrance examination. If that works out, I'll study for four years to get my degree and then find a teaching job. After I start work, I'll save to buy a small house and I eventually hope to get married and have a family of my own. As a teacher, I know I'll never be wealthy but I won't be poor either. I believe I will be content and I know I will have broken free from my family's cycle of poverty. I hope my children will grow up with the determination and confidence to achieve anything they set their hearts on. I will give them all the encouragement they deserve. I will tell them about their grandmother and the sacrifice she made, which wasn't only for me, but for them too. If I can, I'll send a little money home to my father. Despite the problems my parents had, I know my mother would want me to do that.

Subsequently:

Novice Maha Sorasing disrobed after completing his high school studies. He was awarded a scholarship by the

Students' Education Trust and studied for four years for a Bachelor of Education degree in Thai. He then became a teacher at his old monastic school in Nakhon Sawan, where he now teaches Thai to the novices. With SET support, he is also currently studying for a Master degree in Education Quality Assurance.

11

Novice Thanapum

Following in father's footsteps

I consider myself to be a lucky boy, as well as a fortunate novice. At my monastery, every young novice is attached to a particular monk who acts as his teacher and guide. The monk should take care of his novices, set a good example to them and make sure they behave well and follow their precepts. Sometimes, the monk may not do his duty properly or doesn't care enough about his novices, especially if they are often naughty and give him problems. Some novices don't respect their monk or won't listen when he tries to guide them, so sometimes the relationship isn't always good. I consider myself lucky and fortunate because, in my case, my own father is my teacher-monk. He takes his duties seriously and cares about all the novices in his charge, not just about me.

My father has been a monk for fourteen years, since he was twenty. I respect and admire him very much and I think he's a good monk, but I'm not saying that just because he's my father. I think he's a good monk because he really seems to understand the Buddha's teaching and tries to follow it in every moment of his life. He gained that understanding in the best possible way; by learning from his own life and past experiences and by relating them to the Dhamma.

Immediately before he ordained, my father was a very unhappy young man. When he was nineteen, many problems suddenly came into his life. He'd married when he was very young and already had a wife and a three-year-old son – that was me – and he was halfway through a college course studying agriculture. He loved farming and was studying because he wanted to learn not only how to get the best from his family's land and improve the crop, but also how to care for the land properly so that it would remain fertile and continue to support the family. One night, my father was involved in a road accident and suffered terrible head injuries. He was in a coma for about six months. His family thought he would never recover, but he did, suddenly and unexpectedly. Unfortunately, during the months that my father was in hospital, my mother met another man and disappeared from our village with him, leaving me, her only child, with my father's parents. I haven't seen my mother since then. I suppose she thought my father wouldn't recover and that she wouldn't be able to take care of him, or me. I'm not sure how old she was, but I think probably only about eighteen or nineteen, so maybe she was scared of the responsibility. When my father finally returned to the village, he discovered that he no longer had a wife or home, his college place had been lost, and his life had completely changed.

It took my father a long time to get over the shock of his new circumstances. When he did, he decided to ordain as a monk, intending to stay in the robes for the rest of his life. He knew that before he settled down to live in a monastery, he first had to overcome the anger and bitterness he felt about what had happened to him. In Buddhism, we're taught that such strong and unwholesome emotions prevent spiritual development and progress. Obviously, you can't develop true compassion for others, or learn how to always have a calm mind, if you are carrying bad feelings like anger, hatred or bitterness around with you. Those feelings come from *jai rawn*, a hot heart, but Buddhism is about keeping *jai yen*, a cool heart. Buddhism teaches how to observe the mind and emotions and how to control them. My father understood that very well so, after he ordained,

205

he became a wandering monk, living in remote forests and caves and with little contact with people.

It's an ancient tradition for Buddhist monks to wander in forests and lonely places, but not many do it any more. These days, I think the majority of monks spend most of their time in the study of Buddhism, rather than in the practice of Buddhism. A famous old Thai forest monk said that's like keeping chickens in the back yard and going round collecting their droppings instead of the eggs. But my father wanted to practise in the old way, so he wandered in the forests and spent a lot of his time in meditation, trying to understand himself and the unhappiness he had experienced. He wandered for three years and I never saw him during that time. When I did next see him, he had changed completely and seemed calm and happy. He finally decided to settle down in a monastery in his home province of Nakhon Sawan, which is where we both now live.

After my father ordained as a monk, I stayed with my grandparents. I lived on their farm, which was in a small, isolated village on the edge of a reserved forest. The land was very fertile and my grandparents grew corn, cassava and rice. As I got older, I very much enjoyed working on the farm with my grandparents, especially during harvest time. We all worked together to get the harvest in and there was always a good feeling at the end of the day when we went back to my grandparents' house for dinner, tired and hungry, but knowing we had done a good day's work. I especially liked working on the farm after my aunt taught me how to drive the tractor. I was only about ten, so driving was very exciting and great fun for me. I wasn't very good at first, but my grandparents never shouted at me when I drove the tractor straight through the corn, or into a ditch. Besides helping on the farm, I had my daily duties around the house too. I collected firewood from the forest, carried water from the well and helped my grandparents as much as I could. I even cooked sometimes, but my grandmother got bored with fried eggs, which were my favourite and the only thing I could cook, so she took over the kitchen again.

Although I was happy living with my grandparents, I missed my mother and father constantly and I sometimes felt quite sad and lonely. When I was a small boy, I never stopped hoping that my mother would come back some day. If she came back, I thought my father would disrobe and we could all be together again. In the first few years after my mother left us, I sometimes walked to the edge of the village and stared along the track, hoping to see her walking towards me. I was always disappointed when she didn't come. When I got home, my grandmother would hug me and tell me that I should try to forget my mother, but I always thought that maybe she would come the next day, and that I shouldn't give up hope. I'd still like to see my mother, but now I'm content with the ways things have turned out for me. I hope they've turned out well for her too.

The village where I lived with my grandparents was very pleasant. There were less than a hundred houses and only about three hundred people, but it was neat and tidy and there was a good community feeling. There were hardly any problems in the village. I don't think any of the young people took drugs, or got into trouble with the police. That's quite unusual these days, but I think the remote location and living near to the forest had a lot to do with it. Because the village was on the edge of a forest, there was a feeling of being close to the traditional Thai way of life, which in country areas is very simple, or used to be. The forest was under the protection of the Forestry Commission, but the villagers had an arrangement with them that the community would look after the forest and in return would benefit from all that the forest offered. A lot of our food came from the forest, as well as firewood, building materials and many traditional herbal medicines. For their part, the villagers protected the forest and made sure that the very old trees weren't cut down by illegal loggers, or that poachers didn't kill the endangered animals and birds that lived there. The arrangement worked well. The people in the village really cared about the wellbeing of the forest because it was so important to their own well-being, and to their future prosperity.

I grew to love the forest very much and it became my playground. There weren't any ferocious animals like tigers or bears living there, but in the deepest parts there were enormous boa constrictors and some other very poisonous snakes, like king cobras. I saw them sometimes but I wasn't frightened and they never harmed me, maybe because I didn't try to disturb them. There were many deer, foxes and squirrels in the forest too, and lots of different kinds of wild chickens, which are very different from normal farm chickens. The forest wasn't only a place for me to play. Whenever I thought I had some problem, if I was unhappy or in a bad mood, I would walk deep into the forest and my problems seemed to disappear, or at least didn't seem so important any more. The forest vibrates with harmony and somehow manages to put problems into a better perspective.

Although I often spent hours in the forest in the daytime, I was frightened to go there at night, but not just because of the snakes. My grandparents were very superstitious and often told me about the spirits they claimed lived in the deep forest and guarded it. They told me that before any old tree could be cut down, an axe had to be propped against the tree and left overnight. Next morning, if the axe had fallen over during the night, it meant that the forest spirits didn't want that tree touched. If the axe was still propped against the tree in the morning, it could be cut down. My grand-parents said it was asking for misfortune to cut any tree that the spirits wanted left alone. I've heard that there are even some very ancient trees in Thailand which have been 'ordained' by monks who live in forests. The monks wrap a robe around the tree and that warns ille-gal loggers off. I don't think any logger would dare cut down a tree which had a monk's robe wrapped around it. My grandparents told me that most of the spirits in our forest were good but that sometimes a bad one might be lurking there too, just waiting to grab a naughty little boy like me. I know now that wasn't true but at the time it frightened me, so I always tried to be a good boy.

I never saw a ghost or spirit in the forest myself but I started to believe my grandparents after a very scary thing happened to my aunt, when I was about eight. She'd been in the forest one evening to collect herbs but when she came home she acted as though she was drunk, although she never drank alcohol. She fell on to the floor and started writhing around and rambling on about things we couldn't understand. My grand-parents said my aunt must have been possessed by an evil forest spirit. We were all very frightened and didn't know what to do, so my grandmother sent me running to fetch an old man from the next village, who knew a lot about spirits. The old man put a white cloth over my aunt's body and chanted for a long time. Gradually she became calmer, until after about an hour she became still and finally fell asleep. When she woke up, she couldn't remember anything that had happened to her from the moment she went into the forest.

My father isn't superstitious at all and he has studied plants and trees. He doubted that my aunt was really possessed and said that she might have touched or eaten some poisonous plant that caused her to become delirious for a short time. Even so, I remained scared of the forest at night for a long time, until I started to learn Dhamma. Now, I think if you understand and follow Dhamma, that's a protection against all sorts of evil things, whether they are real or just imaginary. I'm not frightened of the dark forest any more.

I'm sorry that so much of the forest in Thailand has been cut down, especially as it's mostly been cut for the benefit of just a few greedy people. For centuries, the forests played an important role in our lives and I think Thai people lived more in harmony, not only with nature, but also with themselves and with each other. Now, in their big cities and concrete apartments, many people aren't so caring towards each other and are very selfish. They take all they can, all the time, without giving anything in return. The people who are happy to see the forests cut down, or replanted with commercial tree farms, are probably people who have never lived close to a forest and haven't experienced the peace of mind or feeling of natural harmony that the forest can give. For those greedy people, contentment seems to mean having a pile of money in the bank or being more powerful than others in society. That's not the teaching of the Buddha, so I think they have the wrong outlook. I feel sorry for them. There's a lot to be learned from the forest. Living close to the forest and relying on it teaches you to be less greedy. The forest can provide so much but you take only what you need and nothing more.

On his visits to our village, my father and I would sometimes walk deep into the forest and he would teach me about the trees, flowers, animals and birds that lived there. He also explained the Buddha's teaching to me during our walks. The peaceful forest seemed the perfect setting for those lessons; much better than a classroom because the Buddha lived most of his life in forests, bamboo groves and other natural places. Because my father had wandered for three years in the forests as a young monk, I felt he had really come to an understanding of what the Buddha taught and that the forests had helped make him wise, as well as content. My father never put any pressure on me but I was sure, even as a little boy, that I would follow in his footsteps and become a novice monk some day.

Most of the Buddha's teaching isn't really complicated, but sometimes it's hard to see the truth of it for yourself, especially when you are still young, like me. Children are usually happy and carefree because they have so many interesting things to do and enjoy. They forget the bad times as soon as the next game comes along. They don't always learn from the unhappy things that happen to them, or sometimes not quickly. My father taught me to look at my own life, even though I was still young, and to remember some of the unhappy things I had experienced, even if they weren't big or important. He encouraged me to try to relate them to the Dhamma, especially to what the Buddha called The Four Noble Truths, which are about the mental suffering or unhappiness that people cause to themselves and how that suffering comes about. Mostly, we suffer because we always want things to be perfect and we want to have all our dreams and ambitions fulfilled.

For example, I had a dog from the earliest time I can remember. His name was *Namkarng*, which means 'Misty' in Thai. Misty had always been my companion when I walked in the forest. He died when we were both aged eleven. That can be a very upsetting thing to happen to a young boy, but because I already had a good understanding of the Buddha's teaching about Dukkha, or suffering, I knew the sadness came from my own mind because I didn't want Misty to die. I wanted him to stay alive and be my companion for ever. That's an obvious impossibility, but when we want something so badly, we somehow manage to convince ourselves that it can happen, so we only cause more suffering for ourselves when things don't turn out as we want them to. Even though I was upset when Misty died, because of my father's teaching I was able to accept his death as the way things have to be. Being sad was natural but it didn't help bring Misty back to me, so there was no point in causing myself more problems or suffering by wishing he hadn't died. When Misty died, I just took him into the forest and buried him there, without tears, and came away with happy memories that will always stay with me. My father's Dhamma lessons also helped me see why people change as their surrounding conditions change, so that even helped me understand why my mother left us. I think I'm very lucky to have had the opportunity to be taught Dhamma when I was so young. I know I will remember my father's lessons all my life, whatever I do and wherever I go.

My father was pleased that I wanted to ordain as a novice but he thought it best that I should first complete my primary education at a government school, which I did. My grandparents weren't wealthy but they weren't really poor either. I think they could have afforded to send me to a government high school after I finished my primary studies but I decided myself that I would rather ordain as soon as possible and carry on studying in a monastic school. Although I loved my grandparents very much, I also wanted to be near my father so that he could take care of me. I know he wanted that too, because I was his only child. I think of my grandparents a lot and I miss working on the farm, but I'm able to visit them about every two months. I think they are very pleased that both their son and their grandson wear the robes.

I ordained as a novice at my father's monastery when I was thirteen. That was two years ago and I am very happy. I see my father every day and he is always there if I have a problem, either with my life as a novice, with understanding Dhamma, or just with the ordinary problems that young boys face. As well as teaching me about Dhamma and how I should practise as a novice, he also teaches Science at the monastery high school.

Although my father wants me to be a good novice, he's also a realistic man, especially when I break a rule or precept. I think he understands that all young boys get hungry in the evening so he doesn't scold my novice friends or me when we sometimes eat a little food. He doesn't approve though, and always gives us a lecture. He thinks it's important that we should understand the rules and precepts, and not just follow them blindly. He told us that people in India at the time of the

Buddha were very poor and couldn't afford to give the monks enough food for two or three meals every day, so the Buddha made the rule that his monks couldn't eat after noon or in the evening. I think in those days the monks only ate once a day, in the morning, but now most monks eat twice. Also, monks at that time meditated much more than monks nowadays and it isn't good to meditate after eating too much food because you usually just fall asleep. We novices argue that we get given a lot of food by the lay-people, and we don't meditate much, so we should be allowed to eat. But my father explains that following the rule is also a good way of developing the self-discipline that we can use in other ways for our practice as novices. We have to agree, but we still need to eat in the evening sometimes.

Because I live in the same monastery as my father, and in the same room, I have to be very diligent in my practice as a novice. I can't get away with being lazy or badly behaved, like some of the boys in other rooms. Sometimes that's a nuisance, but really I think it's good for me because it's given me a sense of duty and responsibility that I might not have developed otherwise. If I ever feel lazy and can't be bothered walking on alms round, or going to the morning and evening services, my father always wants to know why and I get another lecture. He also makes sure I go to school every day and he won't let me watch television in the evening until I've studied for several hours. Most nights I study until about 10.30pm. Sometimes I think my father is too strict with me, but I know it's for my own progress, so I don't really mind.

My father has his own duties at the monastery school so he isn't always around to check up on me. I do sometimes misbehave and break the training rules by playing football or running about, but I try not to break any of my ten novice precepts. But it's difficult to be a perfect novice and not break a precept sometimes. For example, if a mosquito bites me I automatically kill it, which is against the first precept. I feel guilty when I do something like that, or eat in the evening, especially when a lay-person later pays respect to me. The lay-people bow three times to the monks and novices because we represent the three aspects of Buddhism: Buddha, Dhamma and Sangha. When people bow to me, I feel very ashamed in my heart if I haven't been as good a novice as they expect and I promise myself to try to do better in future.

My father has six novices living in his room. They are good boys and they're all my friends, even though one of them often annoys me by taking my sandals. He doesn't mean to steal my sandals, but he takes them without asking me. I've told him a dozen times that it's against our precept about not taking what isn't given. He says that means not stealing, but my father has explained to me that it also means not borrowing other people's things without asking, in case they get annoyed. Well, I do get annoyed and have to give my friend a kick sometimes, but he still does it. I'll have to learn to be more patient with him, and not get so jai rawn. Although our room sometimes seems overcrowded, it's good fun living with lots of others. The only thing that worries me is that I might get spots or skin diseases from the other boys, but my father laughs and tells me that's not likely. I still worry about it though. I think it's good to live closely with other people, because it teaches you to be considerate and understanding towards them, especially when they take your sandals or give you their spots.

Some of my friends don't enjoy the novice life as much as I do and I think they'd like to disrobe if they could. I know they feel jealous when they see ordinary boys having a good time. Maybe they're jealous because they're too poor to live or study anywhere except in the monastery. I understand their feelings, but I don't feel that way myself because I made my own decision to live as a novice and I'm very happy with my life. I think some of my novice friends don't understand how much advantage they are getting from learning Dhamma at such a young age. Dhamma is so useful in our lives when we get older, so we should try and learn it when we are young. It can help us in many ways, even in something like deciding who is a good person to be our friend. If people follow Dhamma well, they are living life in the best possible way and they must be honest and trustworthy, so they are good people to have around us. People who don't follow Dhamma properly are not such good people. We should be careful of them and not automatically trust them, even if they are important people like politicians, teachers or even monks.

I'll probably become a monk when I reach twenty, but that's a long way off and I'm not sure yet. My father says it's my own decision. If I decide to disrobe after I get my high school diploma, I'll still follow in my father's footsteps and study agriculture. I'd like to work on the land again because I enjoy it. If I had a little land, enough money to build a small house and sufficient food to eat, I think I would be happy. That's more important to me than owning a lot of material possessions, having a high social position or any of the other things that some people dream about. I'm only fifteen, but I already know that those things aren't really important. I don't care about them at all.

Even if I don't become a monk immediately, I'm sure I will at some later time in my life. When I do, I think it will be for a long time, maybe even for the rest of my life. If I was a monk, the first thing I'd do is to wander in the forest for a few years, like my father. I've learned a lot of Dhamma from my father and from books, which is useful, but it's not necessarily the best way. Understanding gained from books isn't always deep enough – it reaches the brain but doesn't always get into the heart. Even though I've had my own father as my teacher, his teaching is still based on his experiences and his understanding, rather than my own. I think living in the forest for a while will give me a much deeper and more personal understanding. I believe that's how my father became so wise, and that's what I want to do.

12

Novice Noom

'A ghost novice saved my life'

By the time I was thirteen years old, I was labouring on a Bangkok building site six days a week, sometimes sixteen hours a day. I was smoking, getting drunk on whisky and taking drugs regularly. In just one year, I changed from a happy and timid little village boy into an unpredictably moody, aggressive and violent lout, and I had started stealing from my friends. If I'd carried on that way much longer, I'm sure the combination of the heavy work, alcohol and drugs would have killed me. It almost did, but I believe the ghost of a novice monk saved my life.

I don't mean the ghost literally saved my life, but that's a possibility too, considering the way I was living then. My life had hit rock bottom and I believe the novice came to me at the moment when I most needed help and guidance. He brought me to my senses and made me understand what I had to do to get out of the dangerous habits I'd fallen into. You may think that's crazy and maybe it is. You may think the whole thing was a drug-induced hallucination and maybe it was. But it doesn't matter now. Real or imagined, the ghost novice made me see the dangerous path I was following and he helped me back on to the right path. I know in my heart I'm not a bad person and I've done my best since I've been a novice to make up for my earlier behaviour and, in a way, to thank my ghost novice friend.

Although I come from a very poor background, I was luckier than many children in rural areas. They sometimes have a much harder time than I ever did. When I was working in Bangkok, I met other boys of my age who'd been regularly beaten up by their drunken fathers or stepfathers, or whose parents were so poor they often had no food to give their children, or simply couldn't be bothered to take care of them. I felt sorry for those boys. They seemed to have had no love in their lives at all and it wasn't surprising that they developed the same bad habits that I did. Perhaps they had some excuse for taking drugs or drinking alcohol, but I didn't. I got into very bad habits at a young age, but I don't think I can blame the poverty in which I grew up, or my lack of education, though I suppose they were both factors. If a child is poor and uneducated I don't think it follows that he or she will automatically become a bad person, or inevitably get into bad ways. It just means they grow up poor and uneducated. I certainly can't blame my parents in any way. They were uneducated and poor, but they were good people and took care of me very well when I was a child. Although we rarely had any spare money, we usually had enough food to eat. Even during the especially difficult times when there wasn't enough food, my parents always made sure my brother and I were properly fed. We didn't have anything in the way of luxuries in our house but we had everything we needed. My father never drank alcohol and he never beat me, except on a few occasions when I probably deserved it. I think I had as good an upbringing as my parents could give me, considering our circumstances.

I was born in a village in Nan Province in the northern region. It was a very small place, just seventy or eighty houses, and all the families were poor. Most of them had only a little farmland but they usually just about managed to get by. Nobody expected to get rich from the land but, if they had enough to eat, I think they were generally content and didn't want much else out of life. That was certainly the case with my parents.

They didn't plan too much for the future because they were more concerned with their immediate situation. They weren't exactly living day to day, but the present problems were always more urgent than whatever might crop up tomorrow.

My mother and father didn't know a lot about Dhamma but they followed the five Buddhist precepts and were honest people. They particularly warned my brother and me about the dangers of alcohol and drugs, though neither was a great problem in our village. Most of the village men drank whisky, sometimes too much, but few of them could be called alcoholics. I think my village was a good environment for my brother and me to grow up in. It was certainly better than some other villages not far away, where they seemed to have many more problems.

My brother was about five years older than me. He wasn't my real brother, he was my cousin, but he was orphaned when he was a baby and had lived with my parents since before I was born. My parents brought him up as their own son and I didn't even know he wasn't my real brother until I was about four years old. Knowing didn't make any difference and I've always thought of him as my brother. When I was still a baby, he took care of me during the day while my parents were working and we loved each other very much. We still do. Because I know he loved me, you might think it odd that it was my brother who introduced me to alcohol and drugs when we worked in Bangkok. I don't blame him for that. Using drink and drugs was simply how most people in our situation survived and I'm sure he thought he was helping me at the time.

I studied at a little primary school in the grounds of a monastery near the village. I think I was a good student, but as far as I was concerned that was all the education I would have. Very few children from my village went on to high school. I'd have liked to study further but for a boy in my situation that was a silly idea and one I quickly put out of my mind. We all knew that after finishing primary school we had to start working immediately, either by helping our families in the rice paddies or more usually by finding a job in the city, so that we could send money home. We just accepted that as our way of life and it wasn't a problem for us. Neither my mother nor father had been to high school but they seemed to have had a happy enough life without much education, so that's all I hoped for too.

After I finished primary school, I helped for a while on the land but I wasn't really needed, so my father decided I had to work in Bangkok. He'd worked as a labourer in the city for a few years when he was a boy and said he'd enjoyed it, but in those days I don't think young people faced the same temptations or dangers, especially from drugs and particularly from amphetamines. They seem to be a fairly new problem in Thailand which I think is connected with the troubles in Myanmar, but I don't know much about the politics of that country.

You shouldn't think my mother and father were bad parents because they sent me to work far away when I was so young. They weren't. My parents cared for me a lot and would certainly rather have kept me at home if there had been some useful or productive work for me to do, but children had to earn money, even when very young, because that was the only way the families could survive. Because my parents had only a little rented farmland, and because they were both young and healthy enough to cope with the work, first my brother and then me were sent to the capital. My brother had already been working on building sites for about four years before I went to join him in Bangkok.

I was both excited and scared of the idea of going to work in the city. Whenever my brother came home for a few days each year, it was obvious how much he'd changed, but not for the better in any way. Even when he was only about fifteen or sixteen, he looked haggard and unhealthy and without the vitality that I remembered from when he was younger. He drank and smoked a lot and I knew he was taking drugs, though he hadn't had those habits when he lived in the village. When he came home to visit, my brother was always careful not to let our parents see him drinking alcohol because he knew it would upset them, and he never took drugs in the village because it was frowned on by most people. Despite my fear of what could happen to me in the city, I told myself that if I was strong enough I could resist the bad temptations. I did – for about two weeks.

In Bangkok, my brother stayed in a tiny room, about three metres square, and it was arranged that I should stay with him. The room was in an old wooden house that had been turned into a dormitory for labourers, with many small rooms thinly partitioned from each other. It wasn't very pleasant but it was all we could afford. To live as cheaply as possible, two other young men also stayed in our room and shared the rent. They came originally from our province so we all got on okay. The room was very crowded with four of us in it, but I enjoyed living with the others. We spoke the same northern language and had a feeling of community, even if it was only within our room. Most of the young men and boys in other rooms came from Esarn, the north-east region, and they usually spoke Laos together. We didn't really mix with them much, though one boy became a good friend, at least until I tried to kill him. I don't think anybody in the house had been to high school, and we all worked on a building site on the outskirts of the city.

The site was to be a hotel and conference centre. My job was to use a machine to bend thick metal rods that helped reinforce the concrete pillars and floors. I'd never done anything like that before but it wasn't difficult and I quickly learned. I also quickly learned to dislike the work, because it was very tiring. I was only thirteen, so I wasn't particularly strong. There were other young boys of about my age working on the site, and a few even younger than I was. I think it's against the law to employ such young children but the site manager got round that somehow by claiming we weren't working full-time. I'm not sure what 'part-time' means, but my working day, six days a week, was from 8am until 5pm, with an hour's break. I got paid 100 baht a day for the basic shift, but my brother got more because he was older and more experienced. Besides working the basic shift, we were also expected to work as much overtime as we could. I sometimes worked from 7am until 5pm, then after a two-hour break carried on working until 1am. That's a long day for a thirteen-year-old and after a couple of weeks I was exhausted.

I was so exhausted with the work and long hours that I decided I had to leave the site. I couldn't go back to the village because there was nothing for me to do on the land and my parents needed the money that my brother sent to them every fortnight. I had to stay in Bangkok, whatever work I did. My brother and I had a big argument about it. He said I had to work on the site because we were earning good money. I told him that if I stayed, I couldn't work so many hours. He insisted I had to work as much overtime as possible because we had a duty to help our parents. I couldn't disagree with that. Then he suggested I take amphetamines to give me more energy to work. My brother took them every day, except Sunday, when we didn't have to work and spent most of the day asleep. We both knew that taking drugs was a bad habit, but my brother wasn't a bad boy. He was taking drugs only to give him the energy to work longer hours, so that he could send more money home to our parents. He worked considerably more overtime than I did and he knew how dangerous amphetamines were, but he was prepared to risk it for the sake of our parents, whom he loved very much. In a way, I admired him for that. I'd guess that seventy per cent of the other men and boys on the site were taking amphetamines too, simply because it was the only way they could get through the day, and especially the long night.

I didn't want to get involved with drugs because my parents had always taught me to avoid them, but my brother put some pressure on me and I gave in. Before long, I was taking amphetamines frequently. I soon came to rely on them and then to crave them. I'd also had my first taste of cigarettes and alcohol soon after I arrived in Bangkok. I didn't like either at first but within a fortnight I was drinking whisky regularly, though never as much as the other men because I got drunk very quickly. All the young men and boys in our house drank a lot and I think most were taking drugs. There was nothing in our lives except work, alcohol, drugs and exhausted sleep. In the year that I worked in Bangkok, I saw nothing of the city except the inside of our house, the building site, and the one-kilometre walk between the two.

If I'd stopped to look at my life, I would have realised that I was already on a bad path. I didn't realise it because even after just a couple of months, I think my brain stopped working properly, as though some part of it had shut down. I became very apathetic and moody and sometimes wasn't able to think clearly even about my daily life, let alone the future. My daily life and potential future were too depressing to think about anyway, so I didn't think about them and perhaps couldn't see how bad my life was becoming, or the dangers I was heading into. Instead, I just went along with whatever was suggested by my brother or our roommates, because that was easier than thinking for myself. I was just existing from day to day, but with no end to that horrible existence in sight; just work, drugs, alcohol and sleep.

I became so mentally lethargic that I stopped caring about myself at all. Even poor Thai people are usually very clean, but because there were so many people in the house, but only one washroom, sometimes I wasn't able to shower properly in the morning. I usually just had a quick wash under a tap. Some days, I didn't even bother with that and didn't shower until my day off, on Sundays. My clothes were always filthy from working on the site, but I was often too tired in the evening to wash them or even change out of them. I'm ashamed to say I became quite dirty and smelly, but I didn't care. I usually only bothered about personal hygiene when my brother or the other men in the room complained. Sometimes, when I saw myself in a mirror, I was shocked at how unhealthy I looked and how gaunt I'd become in such a short time. I tried to avoid looking in a mirror, because I really didn't like what I saw. I was just a child but I was already worn out.

I also started to become very aggressive. That was completely out of character for me because I'd always been a very timid boy in the village. One night, I was drinking in the room of one of the Esarn boys, who was a good friend. I complained that I never had any money. My brother took care of our money and sent most of it home to our parents. He kept just enough back for our rent and food and the essential drink and drugs. I only saw a few baht each week. The boy suggested that I could earn a lot of money if I hung around certain bars in Bangkok's Patpong area. I didn't actually know what Patpong was then but I knew what he was suggesting. Instead of just laughing it off as a joke, I was furious, because I thought he was implying that I was a *katoey*, a lady-boy. For no good reason, I attacked him. I went berserk, like some sort of wild animal, viciously punching, kicking and biting, but I don't think it was really because of what he'd said. I think I was just trying to get rid of the background frustration and rage that were building up in me. I'm very sorry to say that I hurt my friend quite badly. If a weapon had been handy, I might even have killed him. Luckily, my brother heard the noise and came into the room and pulled me off the boy. That wasn't my last fight. If I'd been drinking or taking drugs, I often had furious arguments or fights with the other boys and they started calling me *ba* – mad. Now, I think they may have been right. I *was* going mad, but I didn't know it.

I carried on like that for a year, getting worse and worse in my behaviour. I thought working on a build-ing site would make me quite muscular, but instead I was getting thinner and physically weaker, though more aggressive. I was also becoming careless. I had a couple of quite bad accidents on the site, hurting not only myself but on one occasion injuring one of the other men. I was eating less but taking amphetamines and drinking more frequently. The only time I felt okay even for a short time was when I was drunk, then I could just forget everything. When I was drunk, I never really knew what I was doing, but I didn't care either. One time after I'd been drinking, I let one of the Esarn boys put an ugly tattoo on my arm, which I'm now very ashamed of. I was sometimes so desperate for alcohol or drugs that I even started stealing; something I would never have considered just a year before. If the other boys were working and I was in the house alone, I'd sometimes break into their rooms looking for whisky or amphetamines and even stole money on a couple of occasions. One time, someone came home unexpectedly and caught me going through his things, which later led to a fight between him and my brother and then one between my brother and me. I'd never had a fight with my brother before, but it didn't bother me. Why should it? Fighting had become just one more normal aspect of my life. I was only thirteen, but in one year I'd become a violent alcoholic, drug addict and thief. How much lower could I get?

On the night before my fourteenth birthday, nobody was working overtime and we had a sort of party in our room, though it was just the same as most other nights – drinking whisky, but more than usual. I didn't really want to drink at all that night. I'd had a headache and had been feeling sick and feverish for about two weeks and it was getting worse each day, but the others told me to drink, so I did. One of the Esarn boys wished me a happy birthday and gave me a pill that wasn't an amphetamine. I didn't know what it was but I took it anyway. I've no idea what happened to me that night but when I woke up in the morning, I was lying fully clothed and soaking wet in a garbage-filled ditch behind the house. I'd been sick several times and I felt very ill. My brother found me there and helped me back to our room, though I was hardly aware of anything going on around me.

It was obvious to my brother that I was ill, not just hung-over, and he said I should stay at home that day. I couldn't have gone to work anyway. I was so weak and feverish I couldn't even stand up unaided. My brother laid me down on my sleeping mat, left me a bowl of rice and a bottle of water, and went to work. By 8am the house was deserted and silent. I slept for a time but then I woke up with my body trembling violently, feeling very hot and with my clothes soaked in sweat. My throat was parched but I didn't even have the energy to reach for the water bottle. I just lay on my side, staring at it. For a long time, I seemed to be drifting in and out of consciousness. I felt sure I was dying, but I didn't really care. It was then, when I opened my eyes one time, that I first saw the ghost of the novice. I know I was feverish, maybe even delirious and probably still under the effects of whatever drugs I'd taken, so it could have been a hallucination, but I'm sure he was there.

Normally, I think I'd be very frightened of ghosts, but the novice wasn't scary at all. He was just a thin little boy, standing in a corner of the room, just a few feet away from me. When I first saw him, I didn't cry out in fright or make any movement, though I was too weak to do either anyway. I just stared at him. The novice was wearing a tattered, dark-coloured robe and he looked about the same age as me, or maybe even younger. He didn't move or make any sound. He just stood in the corner looking at me with a sad expression on his face. He looked as though he had been crying and I remember feeling very unhappy – I may even have cried myself. For a few minutes we just stared at each other, then I drifted back into unconsciousness or sleep. The next time I opened my eyes, the novice was still standing in the corner, but he was holding an alms bowl and looking at the floor. After a moment, he raised his eyes and looked directly at me. Later, when I opened my eyes again, he was standing almost next to my floor mat, bending forward slightly and with one hand stretched down towards me. For a moment I was really scared. I was sure I was about to die and that he had come to take me to heaven or somewhere, but then I saw he was smiling. I thought he wanted to help me up off the floor, but I noticed he was holding something in his outstretched hand, which may have been a small piece of cloth. I wanted to reach out my hand to him and to take whatever it was he was trying to give me, but I didn't have the strength. That was the last time I saw him before I drifted off again.

I woke up much later feeling very sick and desperately needing to get to the toilet, which was down the hall. That was too far, so I pulled myself up to a low window and leaned out to be sick, but I was suddenly dizzy from moving too quickly. I fell headfirst out of the window. I landed on my back in the rubbish-covered dirt outside, vomiting over myself. Every part of my body seemed to be burning and I was retching and being sick every few minutes. I'm ashamed to say I had other accidents too, like a little baby, but I didn't have the strength to drag myself off the ground to clean myself up. This is a horrible thing to tell you, but I realised my head was lying in something very nasty left there by a dog, but my head felt too heavy to move, so I didn't. I just lay there on my side for several hours, crying, moaning, shaking, stinking and retching, with an ear full of dog shit. I knew I'd reached rock bottom and was going to die. I just wished it would hurry up and be over. Happy fourteenth birthday, Noom.

It was almost dark before I felt strong enough to move. I crawled slowly to the washroom and managed to get out of my filthy clothes, which I threw out of the window. I was completely exhausted but I cleaned myself up as best I could, then dragged myself on my hands and knees to our room, collapsed on to my mat on the floor and passed out. I was unconscious for nearly two days. When I woke up, the first thing I saw was my brother, kneeling beside me with a water-soaked cloth, trying to squeeze drops of water into my mouth. He started crying as soon as I opened my eyes, because he'd been sure I was going to die. He held a water bottle to my lips and I drank a little, then lay quietly for a few minutes without speaking. Although I was weak, hungry and thirsty, I felt better than I had for a long time, not only because the fever and sickness seemed to have almost gone, but I think I'd vomited all the badness of the alcohol and drugs out of my body as well. Maybe I'd got rid of them from my mind too, because I knew at that moment that a black period of my life had ended. My brother asked me how I felt. I just replied weakly, 'I'm going home' and went back to sleep, while my brother held me.

I went home a few days later, as soon as I felt stronger. It was a long journey on the bus and I was still quite sick, but with every kilometre I became happier. When I arrived home, my parents were surprised but very glad to see me. They knew immediately from my appearance that I was unwell. I told them I'd had a fever, but I didn't tell them about the alcohol and drugs. Apart from being very ashamed of myself, I was worried in case they might have felt guilty about sending me to

Bangkok in the first place, though they had nothing to feel guilty about. I was also worried in case they blamed my brother for introducing me to drugs, but I've never felt that he was really to blame. I also didn't tell them about the ghost novice, in case it frightened them. I hadn't told my brother for the same reason. He is very superstitious and I don't think he would have liked to stay in our room knowing that a ghost had visited, even if it was a friendly ghost.

It took me several weeks at home to fully recover. I was constantly tired and very moody and sometimes I had bad headaches, stomach cramps and dizzy spells, but I gradually got better. I ate enormous amounts of food in that time, so much that my mother laughingly complained she had to work longer hours in the fields just to keep up with my appetite. She took very good care of me and I was happy to be back at home, but I couldn't get the ghost novice out of my mind. I felt very sad for him and wondered why he had died when he was still so young, and why he had visited me. One day, I walked to the nearby monastery and just watched the monks and novices going about their duties. I sat in the temple hall for a while, in front of the big Buddha image, thinking about the past year and about my future. I finally made up my mind what I should do, and then decided to talk about it with my parents.

I didn't know until nearly a year later that my brother

had written to my parents soon after I arrived home. He had explained everything about our lives in Bangkok. He'd admitted that we were drinking and taking drugs and that he had introduced me to both. That was a brave thing for him to do, considering our parents' attitude towards drugs, but I think he was very worried about me and blamed himself for my problems. It was good that my parents knew the truth because when I told them I didn't want to go back to Bangkok they agreed without argument. They said the city wasn't a good place for me. I asked how they would manage without me contributing to the family income. My father simply replied, 'We'll manage', as though the money was no longer the main concern. When they asked me what I wanted to do, I told them I wanted to ordain as a novice monk so that I could study at high school, but also because it was something I felt I needed to do. They were immediately supportive of the idea and encouraged me. As I told you, my parents are good people.

I ordained at the local monastery when I was nearly fifteen. To my great surprise, my brother came home for the short ceremony. I hadn't seen him for nearly a year, since I left Bangkok, and I was amazed at the physical changes in him. He'd put on weight and looked much healthier. He said he was still drinking and occasionally taking drugs, but that he was making an effort to stop. He'd moved out of the old house and was getting some sort of therapy or counselling at a drugs clinic in Bangkok. He told me that our father had written to him, saying he must cut down on the overtime he worked. My brother apologised many times to me for giving me drugs and said that he would never forgive himself for leading me into danger. I told him to forget it; it was the past.

The novice ordination ceremony in the far north is quite a lot different from that in other parts of Thailand. In most regions, when a boy ordains as a novice, he usually just wears ordinary street clothes and the ceremony can be quite informal. In the far north, the ordination is much more elaborate and the boy wears very odd clothes, including sunglasses, a red cloak and a tall pointed hat. In the north, boys are often ordained in a group, so I shared my ceremony with five other boys from nearby villages. Although it was a serious ceremony, I felt quite silly and was very pleased to exchange that costume for the saffron robes of the novice. My first day as a novice was one of the most special of my life. It was a turning point for me, because I knew I'd put all the stupidity and bad habits of the city behind me and was starting to walk a better path.

I felt I'd become a novice for a serious purpose, so I wanted to study as much as possible. I couldn't do that at the local monastery, so soon after I ordained I moved to a large monastery in Nakhon Sawan Province. There, I've already studied for my high school certificate for three years, and I also study Pali and Dhamma, both of which I enjoy. There's really nothing about the novice life that I don't enjoy and I try my best to be a good novice all the time. In a way, I feel compelled to do the best I can. I think I have a debt to repay to my ghost novice friend and I don't want to let him down, but I'm equally determined not to let my parents down, or myself.

In the past two years, many surprising things have happened at my home. I'm not sure how he managed to borrow the money, but my father has rented a larger area of land. He also now has a few pigs and a pond for breeding fish. My father knows he's taking a risk by borrowing money and he told me that he expects to have a difficult time for a few years. He thinks it will work out okay, if not for him and my mother, perhaps for their grandchildren. On his last visit home, my brother and a girl from a nearby village decided they will get married and they plan to work with my parents on the new farm. My brother will be leaving Bangkok soon and returning to the village for good. I was very happy to hear that. Perhaps everything will turn out well enough that his children won't have to go to the city, but instead will stay in the village. Perhaps they'll even have the opportunity to go to high school. I hope so. Maybe I'll disrobe and work on the new farm too, but I don't think I will, unless I'm really needed.

When I reach twenty I'd like to become a monk, certainly for a couple of years but possibly much longer. That decision is nothing to do with my ghost novice friend. It's something I've decided I want to do for myself. I've become very interested in meditation and would like to continue my practice for a while yet. I've been lucky enough to meet an excellent meditation teacher who has shown me how to look inside myself and understand how my mind works and how to overcome unhealthy desires. I've also recently met a monk from a monastery in the northeast. His monastery runs a government-sponsored programme to help young drug addicts. The boys, some of whom are very young, stay at the monastery for a month or more while they receive medical counselling from doctors, together with spiritual support and meditation training from the monks. That two-fold approach to the problem seems like a sensible one to me and it sounds like useful and important work. Apparently, many of the boys go back to using drugs after their programme ends, but some don't. A few even remain at the monastery and become novices. The monk has invited me to visit the monastery and he suggested that the programme is something I could be involved in, because of my first-hand experience of drugs and because of my interest in meditation.

I think I'd like that very much and it would be a good opportunity for me to help other young people.

Maybe, when I was so sick in Bangkok, just being ill might itself have been all I needed to bring me to my senses and get me off drink and drugs. But I don't think so because I was already too addicted. Perhaps my vision of the ghost novice wasn't real and was just something that came out of my own mind, because of the fever or the drugs, so maybe it wasn't necessary for me to become a novice myself. But I believe it was. You may think I'm ba but I believe the ghost novice was trying to help me and visited me because he wanted me to ordain. He pointed me in the right direction at the right time and I'm grateful, because I believe it is the right direction for me. Whether he was real or not, I shall always remember that novice in my prayers.

13

Novice Panya

Learning the hard way

O ne of the first things I learned about the Buddha's teaching was that everything that comes into existence must cease to exist; that everything that is born must later die. Nothing remains the same for more than a moment, even those things that seem to be permanent. If you look at a mountain, it may have stood there for millions of years and appears exactly the same today as it was yesterday, but it's not. Even in one day, sun, wind and rain may all have changed it to a tiny degree as they slowly erode the rock. Little animals burrowing in the soil have changed it, the roots of trees and even of the smallest plants have changed it. It's not the same mountain today as it was yesterday and it will be a different mountain tomorrow.

Other things change more obviously and more quickly, even the things that we desperately want to remain permanent. The people we love start off young and healthy, then they gradually get older, weaker, sicker, and finally die. Our emotions and thoughts constantly change too. One moment our lives seem perfect and we are happy, then the next moment we can suddenly find ourselves in a situation that causes us great unhappiness. Maybe it all sounds very obvious, but it's still a lesson that people have to learn and understand for themselves. It can be a hard lesson to learn. I learned it at a very early age, even before I became a novice and started studying Dhamma. My father taught me, after my mother died.

I was only six when she died. I think she was in her mid-twenties, so she wasn't old and that made her death much more unexpected and more difficult to cope with. I don't remember my mother very well now, but I remember her death vividly. It was quite horrific and very upsetting for my little sister and me. My mother died after being bitten by a rabid dog.

In our village, a bite from a dog wasn't unusual because the dogs weren't really tame and didn't belong to anybody as pets. It's become quite fashionable in cities like Bangkok for Thai people to copy Westerners by owning pedigree dogs, the more expensive the better. I think they've become a sort of status symbol for rich people. I remember reading in the newspaper that someone in Bangkok paid a million baht for a little Chinese dog. That's more money than my father earned in his entire life. But in the countryside, dogs are usually just nuisance animals that are tolerated as scavengers. In most villages, many children are bitten before they learn that they have to be wary of them. I'd been bitten when I was very young but it was just one of the hazards of growing up in a rural village and no different from the risk of being bitten by a snake, or stung by a scorpion. When they're alone, Thai dogs are quite cowardly. You just have to raise a stick or pretend to throw a stone and they will usually run away. It's only when they sometimes get together as a pack of half a dozen or so that you have to be more careful. Rabid dogs are always very dangerous, of course, and quite a few Thai people die every year after being bitten.

The dog that bit my mother was alone and apparently asleep, so she didn't give it much attention as she walked past it. Not every rabid dog froths at the mouth or behaves erratically. Mother said later that the dog looked quite normal, but it suddenly rushed at her and bit her leg, then ran away. The bite didn't seem too bad and nobody even thought about taking mother to a clinic, even though there was one not far away. It was just a dog bite and would heal. It didn't heal, despite the efforts of the village shaman with his herbs, potions and incantations. When my mother first started to become sick, nobody even thought that her illness might be anything to do with the dog bite, which had been almost forgotten.

Now I'm a novice and have studied Science at high school, I realise how misguided my parents may have been to place their faith in folk remedies, rather than modern medicine. But many traditional herbal medicines work very effectively and, in Thailand, continue to be used in rural areas on a daily basis. I don't think people always know how or why they work, but they've been tried and tested over many centuries. Anyway, many poor rural people can't afford to pay for expensive drugs from clinics or pharmacies so they have to make do with whatever they can. Even in the cities, some homeopathic and Thai traditional medicines have become quite fashionable and I'm sure for some illnesses they might be better than modern drugs. But not for rabies. I don't know if taking mother to a clinic or hospital earlier would have done any good, but it was two months after being bitten before she saw a proper doctor. She died in the third month.

Before my mother died we were a very happy family; a very complete family. We had a good life with no real problems. Most of the villagers farmed rice and grew vegetables and I think most managed to make a reasonable income, even if they only rented their land, as my family did. I don't think my family was particularly poor or, if we were, I didn't know it. I suppose it depends how you define poverty. My family rented a few acres of land and we usually earned about 30,000 baht a year from the crop That's not much money but there was always enough food to eat for the six of us who lived in our house. I think if you have sufficient food, clothes and somewhere to live, you aren't really poor.

My father told me that his family had lived in the same house for many generations. It was quite spacious, very old and made of wood, but my father kept it in good repair, so it was very pleasant to live in. The six family members who lived in the house were my two grandmothers, my mother and father and my younger sister and I. We didn't live in luxury and we had no television, telephone, or anything like that, but we had enough money for our real needs. They were fairly basic, because we weren't greedy people and were happy with whatever we could afford and which came from our own efforts. If we had wanted a few luxuries, my father could probably have borrowed money from the bank but he disliked the idea of being in debt. We didn't need those luxury things anyway. What we had in plenty were love and happiness and the joy of being together as a family. To us, that was our real wealth, and we all knew it.

Our village had about 500 houses and was two kilometres from Nakhon Sawan City. Because the village was so close to a major city, it's surprising that we didn't seem to have many of the usual modern social problems there, like drug or alcohol abuse. Maybe a few of the village youngsters who worked in the city took drugs, but it wasn't an obvious problem. I was never even offered drugs when I was a boy and, as far as I know, none of my friends took them or had even been tempted to try. It was a good, traditional Thai village where people earned their living from the land and were content with a simple life. There was a little monastery in the village and the monks and novices seemed well behaved and also lived a simple life, so they were greatly respected by the people. I think I was lucky to have grown up in a community like that and in the midst of a hardworking and caring family.

From when I was aged about five, I worked with the rest of the family in our paddy fields. Even my sister, who's a year younger than me, did whatever she could. We children weren't really of much help then, but working together was enjoyable and even fun, and bound us more closely together as a family. Many families in the village had split up, usually from financial necessity. Sometimes, the parents went off to work in the cities and left their children in the care of grandparents, or sometimes it was the children who were sent away to work while the parents stayed to tend the land. Those families had few opportunities to get back together again, except for a few days each year. But my family was always determined to stay together, live together and work together. Even when I started studying at primary school, just before my mother died, I still mostly looked forward to the weekends when I could be with the rest of the family in the paddy fields. On schooldays, I used to rush home from school and change out of my uniform and into old working clothes, just so that I could help the family. They were the happiest days of my life and remain as my most treasured memory.

My parents had been married for about seven years when my mother died. I think they must have been very happy together because I can't remember them ever having even a small argument. My father drank whisky sometimes, but I don't think he was ever drunk, so he was never aggressive with my mother or other members of the family. He was quite a strict man but he never once hit my sister or me, nor even shouted at us. He left it to my mother to take care of our problems, to make sure we were well behaved and polite, and that we did our small chores. He was always working in the fields from early morning until late evening, so he didn't always have much time to spare for us.

When my mother died it was a big shock, not just

for our family but for everybody in the village, because she was so young. My father was terribly upset by her death but although he naturally grieved for a time, he was mentally very strong. He'd never been a novice or monk so he hadn't had the chance to study Dhamma seriously, but he was interested in the Buddha's teaching and, like many Thai people, he had a natural understanding of basic Dhamma. I'm sure that understanding supported him after my mother's death, because he rallied quite quickly. It was necessary for him to, because the rest of the family needed his strength. I'm not sure that my little sister and I really understood what had happened to our mother, and that was the first time that my father tried to explain the Buddha's teaching about impermanence to me.

My sister and I already knew about death because we'd been to the funerals of a few old people in the village. We'd even seen the corpses, but I think we assumed that only old people died. We'd never experienced a death in our own family, because our two grandfathers died before we were born. My father explained about the uncertainties of life and told me that I should never expect good things to last or stay the same forever, because they never do. If you expect good things to last, you'll only suffer. But he also explained that bad things or bad times also never last. Happiness turns into unhappiness, but that eventually goes too and happiness returns. I think he was quite clever in explaining everything to his sad little son. He explained how the weather and seasons change; how one moment the sky can be black and stormy, but then suddenly the clouds clear away and the weather is fine again. He explained how ordinary things wear out or get broken, no matter how much we love them and take care of them. He told me that people, too, simply wear out and die, or sometimes get accidentally 'broken', just like ordinary things. He talked to me for a long time, until I understood completely. My father wasn't a pessimistic man and always tried to look on the bright side, just as I do now, but there's no point in not being realistic about life. The Buddha taught us to follow the Middle Way in everything and I think realism is the middle way between pessimism and optimism. I'm glad my father taught me about impermanence when I was so young, because it was a good support for me later, when he died.

After my mother died, there had to be changes in the family routine. Although my two grannies were quite old, they were both strong and still very willing and able to work in the fields. Their contribution was necessary and important if we were to continue to have a comfortable life. They knew a lot about rice farming because that's what both had done all their lives, since they were little girls. It had always been my mother who'd taken care of my sister and me so, when mother died, my father decided he had to reorganize the way the family lived. Neither of the two grannies could be spared from the fields to take care of the children, so my father reluctantly decided that we had to be split up. I wasn't happy about that but I accepted it because I understood, even at six, that the needs of the family as a whole had to come first, so change was inevitable. It was another lesson in impermanence. My father decided that I should become a temple boy and live in the village monastery. He didn't want me to ordain as a novice because I wouldn't have been able to work in the fields at the weekends, where even my limited contribution was important and would become increasingly necessary as I got older. Becoming a temple boy simply meant that there would be responsible people to watch over me when there was nobody at home. My father and grandmothers were going to be a lot busier in the fields after my mother died and they wouldn't be able to give me so much attention. I think my father was also a little concerned that if I didn't have someone watching over me, I might start to misbehave or run wild.

Although I hadn't liked the idea at first, living as a temple boy was never a problem for me. I was a sort of 'part-time' temple boy. I had many early morning duties at the monastery, so I usually slept there, but I saw the family every day. I still went to the local primary school and I was able to help in the fields at weekends. But at least I had relieved the family of one problem. I felt more sorry for my younger sister. Father decided that she should go and live in a village a few kilometres away, with our aunt. Our aunt had only one child, a daughter of my sister's age, and she was more than happy to take in my sister. Even though my sister loved our aunt and cousin very much, she wasn't able to see our family as often as I did, so she missed us all at first and was quite unhappy. But she soon settled into her new home. She still lives with our aunt and I think she now considers her to be her mother.

With the two children out of the way, but well cared for, my father and two grandmothers got on with the job of growing rice. Despite my father's understanding of Dhamma, he changed quite a lot after my mother died, though I think that was inevitable. People change as their surrounding circumstances change. My father had always been kind and gentle and that remained the same, but for a long time he lost the almost constant happiness he'd had while my mother was alive. I think he tried hard not to let his sadness show, but I suppose he must have loved my mother and missed her companionship very much. He was still a young man, so really there was no reason why he couldn't have remarried, but I don't think he ever even considered it.

Each of my two grandmothers had lost their husbands and various other family members in the past, so they were very pragmatic about my mother's death. My grandmothers were great friends, almost like sisters, and I think my paternal grandmother was a good support for my maternal grandmother when my mother died. My grandmothers had quite different personalities, but I loved them both very much. My father's own mother was as kind and gentle as my father, so I guess he inherited those characteristics from her. She was always very calm, never got angry, and was always ready to give me a hug or comfort me if I had some childish problem. She enjoyed telling me stories when I was a little boy and was particularly skilled at telling the *Jataka* tales – the stories of the former lives of the Buddha. I loved to listen to her stories, but she was equally interested in hearing about my own childish adventures.

My other grandmother – my mother's mother – was quite different, but just as lovable in her own way. She could be impatient and bad-tempered one moment and then full of fun the next. My paternal grandmother would never argue with anybody, but the other one was a real battler and would fight against any injustice, especially if it concerned her two grandchildren and even if she only imagined it. I would always run to my paternal grandmother if I had some silly childish problem or needed a hug, but I would run to my maternal grandmother if I'd just lost a fight with some other village boy, knowing she would automatically stick up for me.

Although my two grandmothers were so different in their personalities, they were like twins in other ways. They were similar ages and had lived very similar lives. Each had come from a poor farming family, neither had been educated beyond primary school, both had worked in the rice paddies full time from about aged eleven, both had married poor rice farmers and both had been widowed at about the same time. They'd lived at our family house since before I was born and they were inseparable. In a way, my grandmothers epitomized a different, older and more traditional Thai way of life. Both had their silver hair cut in a very short 'mannish' style, which is a centuries-old tradition for rural Thai women, both always wore hand-woven sarongs and white blouses, and both had bright red mouths and very bad teeth from their addiction to chewing betel leaves and lime. I can remember them so clearly, sitting on our house steps in the evenings, mixing and chewing their betel and occasionally screeching with laughter at some whispered piece of village gossip.

Even without my mother and living at the monastery, life for me continued in a very happy way until I was about eleven. I was a busy little boy, doing my chores at the monastery in the morning, going to school all day, then helping at home in the evenings and in the fields at weekends. Life seemed good to me and I'd started thinking that maybe I'd be able to go on to high school after I finished my primary studies, at least for a few years. My father and grandmothers had got into a good routine in the fields and seemed to be able to cope, so I thought that maybe they could manage without me. I mentioned studying at high school to my father. He said it would be a good idea, if we could find the money, so that gave me something to look forward to. Then, very unexpectedly, my paternal grandmother died. She hadn't been ill, but simply died in her sleep, I suppose just from old age. That was a great shock to my father and me of course, but I think it had a much greater effect on my other grandmother. She became quite morose without her friend and would sit on the steps alone in the evening, uncommunicative and lost in thought, chewing her betel and staring at nothing. A few months later, she died too, maybe because she missed her companion so much. My father and I were so upset by their deaths in such quick succession, but it also gave my father some very urgent practical problems too. Both my grandmothers had worked in the fields up to the day of their deaths, but suddenly my father had to do most of the work alone, with my help only at weekends. My father had worked hard all his life and wasn't a lazy man, so he wasn't daunted by the work, but it was an impossibility. I knew he needed my help. Once again, my father had to rethink the future of the family, or what was left of it.

I could take care of myself by then, so I moved from the monastery back to the house. I could have done it years before but I enjoyed living at the monastery and had good friends amongst the novices. Although I was still going to primary school, I worked with my father in every spare moment I had, but it really wasn't enough. My two grandmothers had been of enormous help to my father and without them he was constantly over-whelmed by the work. For a short time, he hired a man to help in the fields, but we quickly started to get into financial difficulties, so the man had to go. Our position had suddenly become quite precarious. After I finished my primary studies, it was obvious I wouldn't be able to study any further, but I was quite happy to shelve the idea. Father needed my help and that had to come first. I suggested that maybe my sister should return home to help us too, but my father disagreed. She'd settled in very well at our aunt's and father thought it wouldn't be fair to uproot her again. Father and I worked together in the fields until I was thirteen, but our financial difficulties gradually became worse, mostly because we couldn't cope with the amount of work, but also I think because the price of rice began to drop.

Many of Thailand's neighbouring countries produce and export rice. If one country has a better harvest than another, that country can reduce the export price of its rice, forcing other countries to lower their own price per ton to remain competitive. Even with subsidies and loans from the government, most of which never actually reach the farmers themselves, the lower price per ton trickles right down to the paddy field level. For the first time in his life, my father had to borrow money. He'd always warned me that it was something I should avoid in my own future. He told me that once you start borrowing money from the government, or anybody else, you can easily find yourself with a debt that's never reduced, never repaid, and which just gets bigger as time goes on. Even with a loan, my father and I simply couldn't survive from growing rice any more. By the time I was thirteen, another rethink about the future was needed.

My father decided that there wasn't a good enough future for me in being a rice farmer and that I should become a novice, so that I could study in a monastery high school, get my high school diploma and then find a regular job. Much as I enjoyed farming, I agreed with him. He decided I should ordain at a very large monastery in Nakhon Sawan City. It wasn't very far from the village, but my father chose it because the abbot had been born in our village and was well known and greatly admired by all the villagers. Meanwhile, my father decided to rent less land, leaving just enough for him to manage alone and producing sufficient to support him without getting into more debt. I moved to the city monastery and became a novice when I was thirteen.

I visited my father for the first time about three months after I became a novice. I'd have liked to have gone home earlier but I was already very involved with my studies at the monastery high school. I was quite shocked by how much my father's appearance had changed in such a short time. He'd lost weight and seemed to have aged several years. I don't think it was the work. I think maybe living on his own and reflecting on the great changes that had happened to the family had made him lose heart to an extent. But he wasn't bitter at all. His understanding of Dhamma still gave him strength, but in just seven years his young wife had died, his mother had died, his mother-in-law had died, his two children were no longer at home, he had lost most of his land and income and he was now in debt. He understood that was simply how his life had worked out and that bitterness wouldn't help, but he told me that he no longer found any real enjoyment in his work. Without a family there seemed no point in the constant struggle to make ends meet. I felt very sad for him, especially as my own life was so good. I was happy living at the monastery, I enjoyed my life as a novice, and I liked studying.

My father told me that, as far as he was concerned, one period of his life had ended and that another would now begin. To my very great surprise, he told me he'd decided to give up farming. He planned to sell the house and everything else he owned to clear his debt and then intended to ordain as a monk for the rest of his life. I'm sure that decision wasn't because of his loneliness and he wasn't looking for an easy way out of his problems. I think he'd given it a lot of thought and really wanted to make merit for his wife and my two grandmothers. Making merit for others, as well as for oneself, is very important in Thai Buddhism, but my father had never been either a novice or a monk. That's quite unusual, because most Thai men ordain for at least a few months quite early in their lives. My father was a very moral man and had lived a good life, but he still felt it was important that he should ordain. I was pleased with his decision, especially because he intended to ordain as a monk at my monastery, so we would be together.

My father became a monk and for a time we were very content at the monastery. We walked on alms round and ate breakfast together, went to the morning and evening services together and we both studied — me at the high school and both of us at the Dhamma school. He seemed to enjoy his life as a monk as much as I enjoyed mine as a novice, though I have to say he was always better at following his precepts than I was. I thought we would have many happy years together but then – another lesson in impermanence. My father became ill with what was thought to be a simple chest infection, but which turned out to be much more serious. Within weeks of becoming ill, he was dead.

I was only fifteen, but I had already lost almost everybody of importance in my life, except for my little sister. All the people I'd loved and relied on were gone and now it was very much left to me to make my own decisions. After my father's death, I laid my grief and self-pity aside as soon as I could. No amount of grieving can bring anybody back, so I just decided to get on with my life. But I also realised how lucky I'd been to have had such a good and loving family, even for a short time. I had a novice friend who'd been abandoned at an orphanage when he was only a few weeks old. Although he'd been brought up there by kind people who cared for him well, he'd never known a mother or father, grandparents or siblings. Compared to him, I'd been very fortunate.

In a way, my father's death gave me much more incentive in my life as a novice. Although I'd been a good student at the monastery school, I'd never been very strict about keeping the ten precepts. I suppose I considered myself as a student who happened to live at a monastery, rather than as a novice monk who was also studying. After my father's death, I decided to try much harder. Maybe it's difficult for Westerners to understand, but by following the novice precepts more strictly and by being a good novice, I could make merit for my parents and grandparents, as well as for myself. That had been important to my father and it became important to me. I realised that by wearing the robes just as a sort of school uniform, rather than as the symbol of a novice monk, I hadn't really been making merit for anybody; I'd just been studying. I wasn't ashamed about that, because I think most novice monks, certainly at my monastery, have the same attitude. Most of us are from poor rural families and just want the opportunity to live free while we study free. That's an accepted tradition for novices in Thailand and I think it shows the compassion of Buddhism and the Thai Sangha. But I realised that I could combine being a good student with being a good novice too. That's what I've tried to do for the past four years. I now pay more attention to my Dhamma studies, with the result that I've gained a diploma, but I also give more thought to how I live my daily life as a novice.

I still can't claim to be a perfect novice, but I've realised how important the training is and how useful the Dhamma will be to me in future years. I'm not at all sure where those years will lead me and I don't want to make any certain plans in what can so obviously be an uncertain world. But I know that whatever I do, I can only try my best within constantly changing circumstances. For the moment, I'll be happy to complete my high school studies and then I'll disrobe. I have no dreams of studying beyond that and I don't necessarily want to go to university or college, though I'd be quite interested in studying agriculture because I always enjoyed working on the land with my family. I don't particularly want to be wealthy, but I'd like to earn enough to cover my basic needs, and perhaps a little more, so that I can afford to own a few nice things. But I will never be greedy in my life. I wasn't brought up to be greedy and I know I can be content with the basics. That's something I learned at home, but living as a novice has reinforced that understanding too. I'm sure that I will ordain as a monk sometime too, to make merit for my family, but that can maybe wait for a while yet.

Although I've learned a lot of Dhamma at the monastery school, I still remember father's lessons the most clearly, perhaps because they were reinforced by lessons from life itself. There are lessons to be learned every day, every moment, but I believe if we truly understand about change, about the impermanence all of things, and don't foolishly cling to anything as having in-built permanence, then we can accept all situations just as they are. We can more easily cope with problems as they arise, and we can live our lives in a much calmer way. I've learned to do that, and I am content with my life.

Subsequently . . .

After completing his high school studies, Novice Panya disrobed. He tried for a time to get a job, but then decided that his future lay in farming. He applied for a place at a government agricultural college and was accepted for a two-year Higher Diploma Course in animal husbandry. After completing that course, Panya went on to study at university for a degree in Agricultural Science, supported by a scholarship from the Students' Education Trust.

14

Novice Aud

'My nightmare past is over'

I suppose I should confess right at the start that I've never enjoyed being a novice. It was my own choice to ordain, when I was twelve, but at the time I was a very unhappy and confused boy. I couldn't think of any other way out of my desperate situation except by becoming a novice. The first twelve years of my life were like a nightmare; in fact I hadn't really had a life at all. Being a novice hasn't made up for that, but it's given me a sort of breathing space and time to think about what I want to do in the future. I'm seventeen now, but I feel my real life won't start until I disrobe.

I find the novice life very restricting, though I realise

that's not an excuse for deliberately breaking the precepts. I wear the robes of a novice, so I should behave as a novice. I know that following the ten precepts definitely makes a boy a good novice, and not following them makes him a bad novice, but I don't think that not following the precepts makes that bad novice a bad *person*. I admit I've never tried hard enough to keep the precepts, so I've not been a good novice, but I don't think I'm a bad boy, not deep down bad anyway. I'm just an ordinary boy, and that's what I want to be.

In my first couple of years as a novice I managed to break every precept, including the one about not taking drugs. I'd taken amphetamines since I was about eight years old and it took me a while to stop after I ordained. I wasn't addicted to them but I took them whenever I could get hold of some. I've totally quit now and will never take them again. I'm not proud of my record as a novice and I don't really have any excuses to offer, except perhaps that my early childhood was very difficult and I had nobody to love or guide me. When I tell you my story, perhaps you won't think too badly of me.

I was born in a village in Burirum province, in the northeast of Thailand. There were about 300 people living there and it was a fairly typical northeastern village; quite small and far from any city or town and with a community which just about managed to scrape a living from the land. It was also typical in that drugs and alcohol were a problem there, though I think the drug problem has become very much worse in recent years. All the villagers grew rice and mushrooms, all the families were poor and a few were doing little more than surviving. My family – which was just my father and I – was worse off than most.

We lived in a very old, one-roomed house. It was badly in need of repair but my father couldn't be bothered to fix it up. He didn't own or rent any land and instead laboured in neighbours' fields for whatever they were prepared to pay him on a daily basis. That was usually very little because he was a lazy man and worked only when absolutely necessary. None of the neighbours liked him very much anyway, though I doubt if they disliked him as much as I did. The money he earned was mostly spent on whisky, which was more important to him than providing food or clothing for me. My father seemed to object to spending even one baht on my needs and the only clothes I had were old ones that I begged from my friends. Because we often had no money to buy food, I ate lizards, rats, ants' eggs and insects, or almost anything I could catch. I know Western people probably think it's disgusting to eat such things, but they form almost the basic diet of many poor northeastern people.

I said my early childhood was a like a nightmare but that wasn't because of our poverty. I had enough to eat, somewhere to live and at least a few clothes. My nightmare was my father's brutality to me. Before I became a novice, I can hardly remember a single day when he didn't beat me. He was drunk almost every day and he beat me almost every day. I'm not talking about the odd slap that most children get from their parents when they've been naughty. My father's viciousness in beating me with a stick or belt, even when I was only five or six years old, is something I will never forget. I wasn't a naughty boy at all and I don't believe my beatings were ever deserved, or perhaps only occasionally. My father told me that my mother died when I was born and for a long time I thought that was the reason he seemed to hate me so much. I thought he blamed me for my mother's death. I started to blame myself too and even came to believe my beatings were justified and deserved. Every time I was beaten, I cried not only because of the immediate pain, but also for the mother I would never know and whose death I seemed to have caused. As it later turned out, my mother's death couldn't have been the reason for my father's brutality towards me. Whatever the real reason, my father was a bad man and I was literally terrified of him. I was little more than a slave for him, sleeping huddled in a corner of the room like a dog, shivering in terror of when the next kick or blow would come. A dog would probably have been treated better than I ever was. That was my life at home for twelve years.

Although I was a very unhappy and frightened little boy at home, when I was away from my father I was quite different. I had friends in the village and enjoyed myself with them, just like any ordinary boy. Our favourite pastime at weekends was to ride buffaloes to fields many kilometres away. We would leave the animals to graze while we swam in the canal, or hunted for birds and small animals, which we would then eat. But even during those happy times, always at the back of my mind was the thought that after our games were over, I would have to return home and face my father. I often dreamed of ways I could escape from him. Once, when I was about eight, I asked him if I could become a novice. I'd seen the novices in a monastery near our village and they seemed to be a happy group of boys. But my father refused to allow me to ordain, saying he had other plans for me.

Because we often had no food in our house, I was sometimes forced to beg for rice from other people in the village. Most people were very kind to me. They knew I had a hard time with my father, but Thai people don't usually interfere in each other's affairs, so nobody ever remarked on my home life. One particular couple was especially kind, although they were very poor themselves. Their generosity surprised me because I knew they earned only a little money from their rice crop and there were ten children in the family, all living at home. The family lived in a small house on the edge of the village. Despite their obvious poverty and the very crowded conditions they lived in, they were probably the happiest family I knew. There was always laughter or singing coming from the house, which made me very envious of them. The only sounds that ever came from my own house were those of my father yelling at me, or of me crying. The children were all at least a year or two older than me, but a couple of the younger ones were my friends at primary school. Though they were so poor and had little enough for themselves, they were always happy to share what they had. My school uniform and most of my other clothes had been given to me by the mother after her own sons had outgrown them. Sometimes after school, one of the children would invite me to the house to watch their old black and white television. I loved going there because my friend's mother seemed to enjoy fussing over me. She knew from my bruises that I was often beaten but we never talked about it. Sometimes, she would gently smooth a cool balm over my legs and backside, to take away the pain of my most recent beating. I felt both happy and sad when she fussed over me, because it was how I imagined a mother should care for her child. I very much missed having a mother of my own to care for me like that.

I think her husband was a good man too and he worked hard on his land. He was always very quiet whenever I was around. That was partly because there was some long-standing animosity between him and my father, though I didn't know what it was about. Like most of the adults in the village, he sometimes drank too much whisky but I never saw him become argumentative or violent with his wife, or with the children. I don't think the children were ever beaten, unless they did something really naughty. He seemed to be a fair man and I wished my own father could be as fair to me. I was quite jealous of my friends, because they had such a good mother and father. The parents had tried to educate their children about the dangers of drugs, though I knew that at least one of the older boys was taking amphetamines. He gave me my first pill when I was about eight years old. When I first started taking drugs, I had no sense of whether it was right or wrong and I didn't care anyway. I just needed something – anything – to give me a temporary break from my fear of my father and his constant abuse.

When I was about nine my father remarried. At first I was very excited about having a stepmother. Although she couldn't be my real mother, I hoped that she might care for me as a mother should – maybe even love me a little – and that my life would improve. I wanted a mother like my friends from the big family had. It didn't work out that way. My stepmother was also a drunk. She didn't treat me badly but she seemed almost completely indifferent to me, at least at first. Although she wasn't exactly unkind to me, I think she may have felt that I was my father's problem, not hers. She never interfered when my father beat me, though she usually left the room, so perhaps she didn't like to see me being hurt. I was heartbroken then that I had not only a father who hurt me so much, but also a stepmother who didn't seem to care about me.

One evening, about a year after my stepmother moved in with my father, I made a big mistake. I came home from school early and went into the house, disturbing my father and stepmother at an awkward moment. I rushed back out of the house, very embarrassed but also very frightened, because I knew that mistake would guarantee a beating. It did; one of the worst I'd ever had. My father accused me of spying on him and my stepmother, and of all sorts of other bad things. He thrashed me with a stick, hurting me badly, then kicked me down the stairs. I ran crying from the house and kept on running until I got to the outskirts of the village.

I sat under a tree in a field for a while, quietly sobbing to myself. I felt miserable and depressed; not really from the beating, because I'd got used to the pain over the years, but because of how wretched my life was. I also felt very lonely. I knew there wasn't a single person in the world who loved me or cared about me. Just a few metres away was the house of that big, happy family, with noisy chatter and laughter coming out. It seemed so unfair that I had no love or happiness in my own life, while others had so much. I turned to look at the house, almost resentfully, and realised that the mother was standing at the door watching me. When she saw my tear-stained face, she looked as though she might start crying herself, but then she beckoned me over. I didn't want to go. I didn't want anybody to see me in such a state, but she came over to where I was sitting, silently took my hand and led me into her house.

Whenever I'd visited the house before, usually at least a few of the family members had been away working in the fields. I'd never once seen the whole family together. On that occasion, everybody was there, all twelve of them, sitting in a circle on the floor with a huge bowl of rice and several plates of fish and curry. It was just an ordinary family meal for them, but to me it seemed like a party. The children eagerly shuffled up to make room for me and I sat down with them. Within minutes my beating and loneliness were forgotten, as I joined in the laughter and infectious happiness. I felt completely at home and was so glad to be part of that family gathering, even if it was to be only for the length of a meal. But then, just as we finished eating, I suddenly and unexpectedly burst into tears, surprising myself as much as everybody else. I was surrounded by all those happy people in a real family environment, something I'd never experienced before, and I think the feeling overwhelmed me. I suppose it was mostly self-pity, but I simply couldn't stop myself from crying. When I started crying, the mother chased all the children outside, then she quietly held me. After a few minutes, she said something very strange to her husband, something like 'the boy ought to be told'. Her husband shook his head and reminded his wife about 'the agreement'. His wife insisted and her husband got up and angrily left the room, but then came back a few minutes later and said quietly, 'Tell him then'.

The mother held my hands so tightly and stared into my eyes so intensely that I felt quite frightened. She looked quite frightened too, and glanced at her husband nervously several times before she spoke. He just stared at the floor. She finally said she had something very important to tell me; something she'd wanted to tell me for many years. She said I might have difficulty understanding the story, but that she thought I was old enough to know the truth. And then she told me. She said that my mother wasn't dead. She said that the man I lived with wasn't my father. She said he and I weren't related in any way. I remember staring at her in disbelief, but I was completely unable to speak. My whole body seemed to be shaking and my head was whirling with so many different emotions. I remember particularly the sudden realisation that I hadn't been responsible for my mother's death; something I'd blamed myself about for years. I thought I might faint but finally, in a trembling voice, I asked who my real mother and father were. She looked at her husband for a moment and then, with tears streaming down her face said, 'We are'.

I was so confused. I'd lived for ten unhappy years believing I was alone in the world, an only child, with no mother and a father who hated me. But all the time my real mother and father were living in the same village with my ten brothers and sisters. '*Why? Why?*' I kept asking, tearfully. They told me the full story, although it was obvious that my father – my *real* father – wasn't really willing to do so. I was their eleventh child and I suppose I was some sort of accident. They loved children but hadn't wanted another, already having a family of ten to cope with. When I was born they were heavily in debt and knew they couldn't afford to take care of me properly. Another child would lead them even further into debt. They hadn't known what to do about the situation and were very worried.

When I was still a very young baby, the man that I'd always thought was my father suggested to my parents that he should bring me up as his own son. He offered to be my legal guardian, providing that the arrangement remained a secret. Just before I was born, his first wife had died, childless. He wanted a son who would eventually get a job to provide him with an income and security for his old age. My parents had rejected the idea, but the man then offered money to help pay off some of their debts. My mother said she hadn't wanted to let me go, but my father had finally and reluctantly agreed. He had little choice, because their financial problems were bad and he had to think of what was best for the whole family, as well as what he thought was best for me. He agreed to let the man take me. At the time, the man wasn't a drunk and seemed quite respectable, otherwise my parents wouldn't have let me go. My parents told me that they'd regretted their action for years, but had agreed with the man that my real parentage would always remain a secret. I'd been bought and sold, but I couldn't be angry with my parents about that and it's not such an uncommon arrangement anyway. Maybe a Westerner might think my parents were heartless or immoral to sell their baby son, but I doubt if there are many Western people who really understand what poverty means, or have experienced it for themselves. I'd grown up surrounded by poverty in the village, so I did understand the problems it could lead to and found it easy to forgive my parents.

It was overwhelming for me to suddenly discover I had a family. Because my parents had told me the story, they decided they should also tell the other children. My brothers and sisters were as equally surprised and delighted as I was because they'd originally been told that the eleventh child had died. That night, I stayed at my parents' house, sleeping with the youngest of my brothers and sisters in a big, giggling huddle. That was the happiest night of my life. I was overjoyed then, because I thought my nightmare life had ended. I thought that because everything had been explained to me and I knew who I was, I would now be able to live permanently and happily with my real family. Unfortunately, my newfound happiness was not to last.

Although our parents forbade it, my brothers and sisters couldn't resist telling the story to their friends. Within a day, my guardian discovered that the secret was out. He was furious, but for once his anger wasn't directed at me, but at my real father. He went to my father's house and they had a terrible argument which soon developed into a brawl. My mother finally separated the two men and got them to sit down to talk about the situation. My parents wanted me to return to live in the family home, but my guardian wouldn't allow it. He insisted I was to live with him as his son, as was originally arranged. I doubt if anybody knew what the legal position really was and there was no written agreement about the arrangement, but the man insisted he was my legal guardian. He threatened to call the police if my father didn't give me back to him. My father was frightened of involving the police and eventually agreed that the arrangement had to continue. The man dragged me crying back to his house.

Because it was such a small village, I couldn't avoid seeing my parents or members of my family almost every day, just as I'd done, unknowingly, for most of my life. At first, I made a point of avoiding them as much as possible, because my guardian was always watching. But over a few months, I gradually and carefully managed to increase the amount of time I spent at my parents' home. I even occasionally stayed there overnight, creeping out of the house after my guardian and his wife had fallen into a drunken sleep. If my guardian discovered that I wasn't in his house in the morning, that would usually earn me a beating when I returned. But I didn't care about the beatings so much any more because I knew I had a real family who loved me, which balanced out the abuse and lack of love from my guardian. There wasn't much he could do about me seeing my family sometimes, but he must have realised his potential income from me might disappear if I got too close to them. A great deal of hatred developed between my two 'families' and there were frequent arguments and fights. I was stuck in the middle.

Although the situation was very unpleasant, I had the great comfort of my mother. Over the next year, I spent as much time as possible with her and I loved her as though she had always been part of my life. In return, she smothered me with love. I think she was trying very hard to make up for having agreed to my 'adoption' when I was a baby and wanted to give me ten years of love compressed into the one happy year that we were together. She succeeded in making it the happiest year of my life. And then she died.

I was still only about eleven, so I'm sure you can imagine the effect that having both found and lost my mother in just one year had on me. I cried for weeks. My father had loved my mother greatly and he was equally upset at the loss. He became very withdrawn, began to drink more heavily and seemed to lose interest in everything, even in his children. He had so many children working on the rice farm that he didn't really need to do anything himself, so he mostly stayed in the house, drunk and morose.

I think my guardian saw that as his opportunity to

break my developing ties with my family. My guardian saw me only as an investment and I would soon be old enough to be sent to the city to work, so I had considerable future value to him. Soon after my mother's death, my guardian went to see my father and claimed that I obviously needed the love of a mother and that I should therefore return to his house to be cared for by my 'stepmother'. He said that it wasn't good for me to have two families and it would be best for me if I wasn't allowed to visit my real family's home. He also reminded my father once again that those were the terms of their original agreement and that he was, after all, my legal guardian. To my great disappointment, my father apathetically agreed and, much against my own wishes, I returned to live all the time at my original home, with strict instructions not to visit my family and not to stay overnight at their house.

I'd just finished primary school then and very much wanted to go on studying to get my high school diploma. I'm not a stupid boy. Even when I was younger, studying had seemed to me the best way to escape from the life that I believed I was doomed to follow: labouring in Bangkok for the rest of my life. I didn't want that. None of my brothers and sisters had been able to study at high school because the family had been heavily in debt for years, but my mother had promised me that she would try to find some way for me to carry on studying. But that was not to be. My guardian decided that I would start work as soon as I turned twelve years old.

Since my guardian had married, things had slowly changed at his house and definitely improved, at least as far as I was concerned. My stepmother was not drinking as much as before and she seemed to have gained some measure of control over her husband. After my mother's death, she even began to take an interest in me. She'd been as surprised as everybody else to learn that I was not her husband's real son. My stepmother couldn't have children of her own and I think that after my mother died she made a genuine effort to be like a mother to me. She cut down even further on her drinking and encouraged me to stop taking amphetamines, which I did. I was really happy that she was taking an interest in me and I wanted to please her.

The turning point in our relationship came when she was responsible for bringing my beatings to at least a temporary end. One evening, my drunken guardian raised his fist to hit me but my stepmother grabbed hold of his arm to restrain him. He hit her in the face instead. My stepmother, absolutely furious, knocked him down with one blow to the side of his head. I nearly shouted in joy! That was the last time my guardian tried to beat me, at least for a while. Although my stepmother could never replace my real mother, I started to like her quite a lot. We talked often and she became a friend to me, or like an older sister maybe. I even began to love her a little and for a time I felt much happier with my life. And then, after about a year, she died too.

Although her death wasn't as shattering for me as the death of my mother, I felt that once again my life had been turned upside down. If anything, my situation was worse, because I was still stuck with my guardian but I now knew that I had a real family. Because of my father's 'agreement', I was forced to live with a man whose main pleasure in life seemed to be in beating me at every opportunity. The beatings had started up again almost immediately after his wife's funeral. After her death, my guardian's plans for my future were brought forward. He intended to send me to stay with his brother in Bangkok immediately, so that I could start work as soon as possible. This 'uncle' had once stayed for a time in our house and he seemed every bit as unpleasant and brutal as my guardian. I didn't know how to escape from the situation. Maybe that sounds pathetic, but I was only about twelve and I was very confused. I started taking amphetamines again almost as soon as my stepmother died, just because there seemed no reason not to.

After I got over the shock of my stepmother's death,

I became determined to find some way out of my situation as quickly as possible. I thought that I could go along with my guardian's plan to send me to Bangkok, but then simply disappear into the big city and find myself some sort of work. But a twelve-year-old alone in Bangkok didn't seem like a good idea. If I simply ran away from my guardian, I would be frightened of ever returning to the village, but I didn't want to lose my ties with my family. I didn't want to work anyway. What I wanted to do was study. I felt that studying was the real escape from what were all unacceptable alternatives. I'd had a horrible past, but I wanted a good future and I knew studying was the only way to achieve that. My guardian certainly wouldn't allow me to study and my father couldn't afford it. My priorities were to get away from my guardian, to study, and to be able to see my family. There was only one way I could see that would achieve all those aims and that was by ordaining as a novice monk. I decided not to wait even a moment.

I went to see the abbot of a nearby monastery and he said I could ordain if I had my parents' permission. Then I immediately went to see my father. He was drunk and depressed, still grieving about my mother's death, but that may have been to my advantage. I didn't mention wanting to study and instead told him I wanted to ordain as a novice so that I could make merit for my dead mother. He became very emotional at that idea and wanted me to ordain very much, but then came back to the agreement he'd made with my guardian. I told him desperately that the agreement didn't matter, because the abbot needed my father's permission, not the other man's. My father was unsure, but I practically dragged him out of his chair and to the monastery. Within hours, I was a novice monk. I would guess that my guardian was furious when he discovered I'd become a novice, but he would have known he couldn't do a thing about it. I had been properly and legally ordained with my father's permission. I felt free. For the first time in my life, I felt free.

Although I wanted to be near my family, I also wanted to be as far away from my guardian as possible, and I wanted to study. Studying was the main priority, so almost immediately after I ordained I moved to a monastery in Nakhon Sawan Province. It was a good monastery with a good school, but I wasn't a good novice, not at first anyway. I was still taking amphetamines whenever possible, though I managed to stop completely a few months after I ordained. Even though I wasn't the perfect novice, I was always a good student. I started my high school studies at the monastery school and I'm doing quite well. I should have my high school diploma within a year. I've also learned a lot about Dhamma and I think that's helped me mature.

Besides giving me the opportunity to study, living as a novice has also given me some structure in my life. When I ordained, for the first time in my life I had very specific rules to follow. Even though I didn't always follow the rules well, at least I knew what they were. They gave me some sort of framework around which I could begin to build my life. I'd never had that before, so that was very helpful to me. I still don't like some of the restrictions of the novice life and I will be much happier to disrobe, but I know living as a novice has been good for me and has helped prepare me for life as a layman.

I've been back to visit my family several times since I ordained. My father has got over his excessive drinking and has recovered from my mother's death. I love my father very much and he loves me. I think we have an ordinary father and son relationship and I really couldn't wish for anything more. A few of my many brothers and sisters now work in Bangkok, but most have stayed to work on the family farm. I'd be very willing to work on the farm after I disrobe, but I don't think I'm really needed full time, so I'm not sure what I will do. I think I'd like to learn a trade or skill and I hope that my brothers and sisters in Bangkok may be able to help me study.

My guardian no longer lives in the village. For a long time after I ordained he tried to cause trouble for my father, but some of my older brothers had become very big young men by then and they suggested to my guardian that he might be happier living elsewhere. He took the hint and disappeared from the village.

Although I can never forget or forgive the brutality I suffered in my early years, I try not to feel too bitter or angry about it. I can't pretend to be grateful to my guardian in any way, but the pain and humiliation I experienced at his hands has taught me to be much more understanding and sympathetic towards other children who might have the same sort of home life. Sometimes I see boys and girls living rough on the streets – some of them no more than eight or nine years old – and I wonder if they may have run away from situations similar to my own. As a novice I don't have much money, but if I have a few baht to spare I always give it to them, or some food from my alms round or, perhaps more importantly, just chat with them for a few minutes. I know, from my own nightmare past, that even a small act of kindness means a lot to an abused child, who perhaps feels totally unloved and alone in the world, and with nobody to turn to. I'm so lucky now. I have a big, happy family, I think I can have a good future, and I am no longer alone.

Subsequently . . .

When Novice Aud completed his high school studies, he disrobed. He was offered a scholarship by the Students' Education Trust to study for a trade at a technical college. Aud decided to study car mechanics but, just before his course started, his father invited him to return home to work on the family farm. Aud has since returned to his village.

15

Novice Bird

Granny knows best

As far as I know, both my parents are still alive, but I think of myself as an orphan. I always have done. I've never entirely understood what happened, but my parents decided to separate just weeks before I was born. My father left the village first and then, almost immediately after my birth, my mother handed me over to my maternal grandmother, before she also left. I'm sixteen now but I've never met either of my parents. I've heard that both have since remarried and I believe I have a half-sister somewhere; my father's daughter by his new wife. I'd like to meet my half-sister very much, but I've no idea where she lives. I hope my parents are happy but I'm not really interested in meeting them now. I wouldn't really know what to say to them.

My mother was a Buddhist and my father was a Muslim, but I don't think differences in religious belief had anything to do with their separation or their abandonment of their newborn son. My grandmother told me that my father's family was quite well off. The parents looked down on my mother, constantly making her feel inferior because she was uneducated and came from a poor background. They didn't think she was good enough for my father and did everything they could to stop my parents' relationship. Maybe that's something my mother and father should have sorted out before they were married and decided to have a baby, but it doesn't matter to me now. I was brought up by my granny and love her just as much as any son could love his real mother. Maybe even more.

I was born in a small village in Ang Thong Province, about 100 kilometres from Bangkok. My grandmother was a widow and lived with my parents, but when they separated and left the village she suddenly had no income and nobody to take care of her, as well as finding herself with a newborn baby to look after. That must have been very difficult for her, because she was then nearly sixty years old and thought she'd retired. She should have been retired, because she'd worked in the rice paddies from about the age of eight. Even before

I was born she suffered quite badly from back pains as a result of her many years of hard labour. She certainly didn't deserve to find herself suddenly responsible for a newborn baby or the other problems that unexpectedly landed in her lap because of my parents' separation. But although granny hadn't had any formal education, as a girl she regularly listened to monks teaching Dhamma and she understood the teachings of the Buddha very well. She seemed to particularly understand the meaning of compassion. True compassion for others often means making personal sacrifice, and that's what granny made for me. After my parents abandoned me, granny could have taken the easy option by putting me into an orphanage, or she could have given me away to someone else to bring up. She knew that wasn't right and was determined to take care of me herself.

I didn't realise until many years later just how much granny had to sacrifice on my behalf. When I did realise it, I became equally determined to take care of her in return, as she got older and her health worsened. I know granny had a constant struggle to bring me up when I was very young. She had only a small piece of land on which she grew a few vegetables and just about enough rice to feed us both. If there wasn't enough to feed us both, she went without. When I was still a tiny baby, she often had nobody to take care of me during the day while she worked in the fields, so she usually took me with her, in a basket. As soon as I was old enough, from about the age of six, I helped her in the rice paddies.

Granny knew a lot about farming and was a good and patient teacher for me. We enjoyed working together very much. As we worked, she would chatter away constantly, telling me about various kinds of vegetables and fruit, the many different types of rice, and how to care for the land; exactly the same things her own mother had taught her when granny was a little girl. We tried our best to get as much as possible from our land, but with a limited area of land there could only ever be an equally limited harvest, no matter how hard we worked. Even with my help, our financial position couldn't improve. We were very poor and sometimes we were hungry, but we managed to survive. Despite our poverty, we had a good life together. I'm sure it was partly our great love for each other that saw us through the most difficult times, but granny's understanding of the Buddha's teaching also helped us then. She often impressed on me the importance of keeping the five precepts and of living a good and moral life, regardless of our personal circumstances. We knew we lived a simple, honest and blameless life, so that was good enough for us.

Granny insisted I should go to primary school, even though that meant she had to do most of the work in the fields on her own. I did what I could at the weekends, but she really needed more help. Over the years, she'd caused quite severe damage to her spine from the constant bending needed to plant and harvest rice. That's a common problem for rice farmers. In rural areas, it's not unusual to see old ladies permanently bent at the hips, quite unable to straighten up. As farmers gradually mechanise their farms, I think that's becoming a less common sight, though rice farming is still very hard, labour-intensive work. Granny and I didn't have a tractor, so even the ploughing usually had to be done by hand, though sometimes we were able to borrow a neighbour's buffalo. Often, when I got home from primary school, I'd find granny lying flat on her back in our little house, absolutely exhausted from working in the sun all day. Granny was a very brave woman and never complained about her back pains or tiredness, but instead always smiled and pretended that she was just having a little rest. I felt very sorry for her and tried my best to make her life easier. I even suggested I should give up primary school so that I could take over the heaviest work in the fields, and I meant it. I've always been quite big and strong for my age, so I knew I could do the work, but she was adamant that I should continue with my education. I think she'd never quite forgiven my father's parents for their attitude towards our family because of our poverty, so maybe she was determined that I should make something of myself by studying.

Although life was often difficult, we just about managed to cope for the first eleven years of my life, until I finished primary school. I'd already decided that I wouldn't bother with high school and instead intended to take over all the work in the fields, so that granny could finally retire. She'd worked hard for eleven years to bring me up, feed me and care for me, and I felt it was time I started to repay her for those years of kindness and unselfishness. Granny wouldn't hear of it. She told me she knew what was best for me and she wanted me to go on to study for at least the first three years of high school to get my certificate. If possible, she wanted me to complete all six years and get my diploma. I tried to argue with her but I'd never once won an argument with granny and she wasn't about to let me start, so I had to give in. Really, I wanted to study too, but I still felt very guilty that it meant granny had to carry on doing most of the work in the paddy fields for another three years. I started my first year of high school and thoroughly enjoyed studying. I tried hard at my studies, because it seemed a way of repaying granny. She was always very pleased if I managed to get good marks in my class tests, so that was an incentive for me. It was a struggle sometimes, but we managed to find the small expenses needed for my education for about a year, but then our situation suddenly became much worse. After my first year at school, Granny's health started to deteriorate very quickly. Some days she could hardly walk, and she fell over a couple of times. Despite her arguments to the contrary, it was obvious to both of us that she wouldn't be able to continue working at all for much longer. Although I was quite prepared to leave school, she remained adamant that she would find some other solution to our problems. She did, but it was to lead to two very unhappy years for me.

Granny's first priority, as always, was to see that I was taken care of. She wrote to my father's sister, who lived in Chonburi Province. Chonburi is about 160 kilometres from Ang Thong. I'd never met my aunt or any members of my father's family, but granny knew my aunt slightly from when my parents were married. My aunt wasn't exactly rich, but she certainly wasn't poor. She owned a large area of land on which her family grew potatoes, soybean and other vegetables. I don't know what had happened to her husband, but she had three sons, all a few years older than me. She could easily afford to pay for them to study at a good high school and she also employed a couple of people to work in her fields.

Granny told my aunt in the letter that it was about time my father's family took some responsibility for me and that they should help towards my future. Granny asked for nothing for herself, but explained that she had done her best for me for twelve years and that her health was failing. She almost begged that I be allowed to live in Chonburi with my aunt and be able to continue studying. My aunt wasn't pleased with the idea at first but after several exchanges of letters finally agreed to take me in, at least until I finished the first three years of high school. Fees don't have to be paid for the first three years anyway, so really all granny was asking for was that I should have somewhere to live and someone to take care of me. That was settled and I was to go and live in Chonburi with my aunt and cousins.

Granny's plan for herself was that she would live the rest of her life in a monastery as a *maichee*, or nun. 'Nun' isn't really a good translation from the Thai, though it's the usual one, and I should explain that nuns in Thailand aren't the same as those found in some other religions. In Thailand, maichee wear white clothes and live under eight precepts. Most Buddhist lay-people in Thailand follow five basic precepts, but both men and women sometimes increase their precepts to eight on Buddhist holy days or on other special occasions. On those days, they might stay at a monastery for as little as a day, listening to Dhamma talks from the monks, or practising meditation. The eight precepts are the usual five, but additionally include precepts not to eat between noon and the following dawn, not to seek entertainment or try to beautify the body, and to live without unnecessary luxury. Besides those people who take eight precepts just on special days, there are women who choose to live full time at a monastery as maichee.

Maichee follow the eight precepts all the time, most shave their heads every month and they are often as strict in their practice of Dhamma and meditation as some monks; more so in some cases. Sometimes, older women become maichee because they have nobody to look after them in their old age, younger ones may have suffered abuse, or they may need a safe refuge for some other reason. Some women who become maichee have a very strong desire to follow the Buddha's teaching as strictly as they can and to live in a monastic environment. Even though some are very committed in their practice, the maichees' place in Thai Buddhism is quite lowly and they don't usually receive anything like the same respect as the monks, or even the novices, though there are some famous and well-respected maichee. There aren't that many monasteries in Thailand that accept maichee into the community of monks and novices, but a few do. There are even a very few communities established especially for women, which have no monks or novices in residence at all.

Granny wrote to the abbot of a monastery in Nakhon Sawan Province. The monastery is well known for its maichee community and has established a section in its huge grounds especially for women. The monks aren't usually allowed into that section and it's run almost as a separate little monastery. It even has its own small chanting hall. About forty maichee live there permanently, each in her own tiny kuti. The abbot is very sympathetic to the plight of women with difficulties, especially older women who have nobody to care for them. He is always ready to help if he can. He told granny that she could live within the maichee community, but because the maichee are a drain on the monastery's limited resources, each has to pay 300 baht each month for their accommodation, and for electricity and water used. That's really very inexpensive. To rent even a small student room in the city costs about 800 baht a month, without the additional expenses. The monastery has to find the money to run two huge schools, to pay teachers and to take care of hundreds of monks and novices, so the maichee have to cover their own costs. Granny was able to raise some money by selling her house and land, at least enough to cover her expenses as a maichee for a couple of years, and she made the move to the monastery.

Saying goodbye to granny after twelve years together was a terrible wrench for me. I'd seen her every day of my life and she was the only mother I'd ever known. As far as I was concerned, she'd been the perfect mother. She had never once shown anger or even impatience towards me and I treasured her almost constant smile, her kindness and her wisdom. We loved each other dearly and I could hardly imagine life without her. Not only was she moving to Nakhon Sawan, I was going in the opposite direction to Chonburi, and both of us faced completely new lives within new families and new environments. Although we knew we wouldn't be able to see each other very often, both of us realised that granny's plan was best for both of us. I would be cared for by my aunt and could continue my education for at least two more years. Granny wouldn't have to labour all day in the fields any more and would soon make friends within the maichee community. It seemed a good plan. Neither of us had reckoned on my aunt's attitude to her impoverished nephew.

I'm grateful that my aunt was prepared take me in and send me to school, but I don't think her decision was based entirely on any great sense of compassion or family commitment. I believe she got the best of the arrangement. I've never told my granny this, but I quickly realised that my aunt saw me as little more than a house servant and as a labourer in the potato fields. It was clear from the first day I arrived that my aunt didn't like me, didn't want me and didn't much approve of 'poor' people at all. Nor did my three cousins. I had optimistically thought we would be friends and would be like brothers, but to them I was *sudra* – low caste – and they never let me forget it. That seems to be quite a common attitude amongst some Thais who maybe haven't had personal experience of poverty, hunger, or lack of opportunity. They look down on the poor and uneducated and consider them as second-rate people, which is unfair. I was sometimes very uncomfortable with the family's attitude to me. Snobbery was something I'd never experienced before, because I'd grown up surrounded by people who were all equally poor. I realised for the first time why my mother and father may have had difficulties.

Unfair or not, that's the situation I found myself in, so I just had to make the best of it. If I had to be a servant and a labourer for a couple of years, and be constantly sneered at because of my lowly background, so be it. But for two years, I was very unhappy whenever I had to be with my aunt or cousins. That wasn't too often, as I didn't usually eat with the family and had little or no part in their activities. Although my cousins obviously didn't like me, that was okay because I didn't like them very much either. At least one of them was taking drugs and they all seemed to have a bad attitude, not just to me but to the world generally. They were very spoilt and my aunt gave them anything they wanted, but they were never satisfied. I felt sorry for them more than anything else. Anyway, I shouldn't criticise them too much and will just say that they made my life quite miserable for two years.

I wasn't constantly unhappy, though. Once a week, my aunt allowed me to go to the nearby monastery, where I would renew my five precepts and listen to a Dhamma talk from one of the monks. I met some excellent teachers at that monastery and their talks were a good reminder about how I should live my life. One of the last things granny had said to me when we parted was that I was to try to be a good Buddhist and to keep jai dee, a good heart, regardless of whatever situation I found myself in. That's what I tried to do when I lived with my aunt and cousins. It really did help me cope. I was most happy when I was labouring in the fields at weekends, because I enjoy working on the land, and I was also happy studying at my new school. However, as I neared the end of my first three years of high school, my aunt made it obvious that she wasn't prepared to spend any money on me by paying the fees necessary for the remaining three years. I would have liked to continue studying, but it was simply out of the question.

I knew I wouldn't be able to get much of a job with only a certificate for three years of high school study. I'd be able to find work, but I'd have preferred to study for a career or skill of some kind. A teacher at my school told me that with my three-year certificate, I could study free for another three years at a government agricultural college, where students also receive free food and dormitory accommodation on campus. Because I'd worked in granny's rice fields and had also gained experience of growing potatoes and other vegetables, I'd become interested in agriculture. The farming life quite appealed to me, even though I knew it would never make me wealthy. I thought about talking it over with granny but then, at about the same time that I finished my three years of high school, another problem came up. Granny wrote to me to say her money was running out and she was becoming worried about the future. I found out later that she'd given a lot of her money to help some of the other poor and aged maichee at the monastery, which was very typical of her. She said she still had enough to pay for her accommodation for a while, but would soon have difficulty with other expenses, including buying food, her white clothes and other necessities.

Besides frequently writing to each other, I'd visited granny a couple of times at the monastery. I liked to go during the New Year festival, so that I could follow the Thai tradition of kneeling at granny's feet and pouring a little scented water over her hands, which is a way of showing respect to older members of the family. In return, she would gleefully pour a whole bucket of water over my head, but that was just for fun. I used to stay overnight at the monastery when I visited and one time granny introduced me to the abbot. I liked him immediately.

He seemed to like granny very much too and said she was a real asset to the maichee community, because she was so helpful and kind to everybody.

When granny wrote to tell me that her money would soon be gone, I had to decide what my priorities were. I was sure the abbot wouldn't actually evict granny but the rules were quite strict and the maichee were expected to pay for their accommodation and to support themselves financially. I decided I had only one priority; to repay granny for all the years she had unselfishly devoted to me since I was born, and for all the love she had given me. There were two ways I could do that. I could forget about attending an agricultural college and instead get whatever work I could find, or I could become a novice at granny's monastery. If I became a novice, I could live free at the monastery and continue to study at its high school. I would also be close to granny and be able to take care of her. There was still the very important question of the money, of course, so I wrote to the abbot to ask his advice.

I think the abbot is an extraordinarily wise and compassionate man. He agreed that it would be a good idea for me to become a novice to continue my studies and he said I would be welcome to live at his monastery. The monastery has an excellent high school, as well as a very good religious school. In his letter, the abbot also told me that a monastic fund had been set up by lay-people to be used to help novices in particularly difficult circumstances, especially those who were orphans. I wasn't technically an orphan, but I'd been abandoned as a baby and also had responsibility to support my grandmother. The abbot decided that I fitted the bill for a small, regular grant from the fund. There were no conditions attached but he said he expected me to repay the kindness of the lay-people who supported me, by being a diligent novice and student. I was overjoyed when I received the abbot's letter, because it seemed to be the perfect solution to both my own and granny's problems. Almost immediately after receiving the good news from the abbot, I said a very sincere and permanent 'goodbye' to my aunt and cousins and journeyed to my new home in Nakhon Sawan.

I really do consider the monastery to be my home and I'm very happy living there. I've made some good friends amongst the other novices and a few have become like brothers to me. There's certainly no snobbery or rivalry between us, because most of us are from equally poor backgrounds. I see granny every day and I'm able to take proper care of her, so I feel as though I'm living within a family environment. Although I have to go to the monastery high school and the Dhamma school most days, granny and I still manage to spend a good part of every day together. After walking on alms round each morning, I share my collected food with her and a few of the other older maichee, then later in the day granny prepares lunch from the left-over alms round food for myself and some of my novice friends. Some of my friends haven't got mothers or fathers and granny enjoys taking care of us as much as we enjoy taking care of her. Although monks aren't usually allowed in the maichee section, novices with relatives there can visit whenever necessary. Every evening, after I've finished my homework and duties, I always try to spend an hour or two sitting with her, just chatting. Granny's back gives her less pain now than when she had to work so hard in the rice paddies, but her health generally isn't very good and is slowly declining.

Granny's more than seventy now, but that doesn't stop her leading a very active life at the monastery. She enjoys making a contribution to the community and she's always ready to help with any light jobs that need doing around the maichee section. Many of the maichee at the monastery are about the same age as granny, so she's made a lot of friends. She has also met some very good Dhamma teachers amongst the other women. Granny would be the first to admit that she became a maichee because of her ill-health and resulting difficulties, rather than for religious or spiritual reasons, but since living at the monastery she has developed a deep and genuine interest in the Buddha's teaching. She works hard at making the Dhamma part of her every-day life, though I think she's always done that anyway. The result is very obvious to everybody who meets her.

Although my own reasons for becoming a novice weren't much to do with religion either, I believe that ordaining has also helped me in more than just the practical ways I originally hoped for. On a practical basis, Thai lay-people are often very kind to monks and novices, particularly to the younger ones who've come from poor backgrounds. The people are very generous in offering money to help us buy books and the other things we need for our studies, as well as for our daily needs. Because of their generosity, I don't have to worry about food, clothes, accommodation or education costs, and any spare money I have I give to granny for her needs. I try to repay the lay-people's kindness, as well as the abbot's compassion, by being the best novice that I can be. I'm a sixteen-year-old boy, so a few of the precepts are difficult to keep, though I find others very easy. I've never deliberately killed anything, I've never even been tempted to drink alcohol or take drugs and I've never stolen anything.

Even if I'm not very successful at keeping all the novice precepts, I try to be a good Buddhist by follow-ing the Dhamma and making it part of my life. The Dhamma I've learnt in the last couple of years is defi-nitely helping me to become a better person with a good outlook on life. I don't mean that my outlook before I ordained wasn't good, or that I was a bad person, but we can all aim to be better. I believe that living the Dhamma and using it in our daily life is the best way to do that. Living as a novice and studying Dhamma has taught me that a simple life is also the best life and I think it's given me a very uncomplicated outlook. I really don't want a great deal from life, or at least, not in the way of wealth or material things. I want contentment, a sense of wellbeing, and the knowledge that I'm living my life in the best way I can. I've never had wealth or any material things anyway and I've no desire to start accumulating them. As a novice, I have everything I need for my wellbeing, and little else. I do have an old radio, but that's my only possession apart from things like my robes and alms bowl and the few other things I need to live my life as a novice and student. Maybe my simple outlook on life might seem unimaginative or lacking in ambition to some Westerners, and perhaps even to some modern young Thai people like my cousins, but that's how I look at things.

As for what I'll actually do in the future, quite honestly I hardly give it a thought. I still have a couple of years to go before I finish my high school studies. I'll be eighteen then. Most novices disrobe and start work as soon as they have their high school diploma, but I may remain as a novice and then perhaps even ordain as a monk when I'm twenty. Really, everything depends on how much granny still needs me, because as far as I'm concerned my duty is to take care of her for as long as necessary. Thinking about my own future can wait awhile, until the proper time. Like most Thai people, granny has a healthy and pragmatic attitude towards dying. It's not something she fears and, as always, she's more concerned about my future than her own. During our evening chats, she sometimes asks me what I'll do after she's gone. I tell her that I'm really not sure, but that I still have it in mind to study agriculture. I don't have any land of course, but maybe if I worked for somebody else for a while and carefully saved my money, I might eventually be able to afford to rent a small piece of land to get me started. Granny thinks I'm daft to want to do that, but to her farming equates with poverty, because that was her experience. I tell her, as usual, that she knows best and we drop the subject, but I think her own family's poverty – which goes back many generations – was really to do with lack of education. I'm sure with a sound education in agricultural science, I could make a reasonable success of farming a small area of land.

Although I'm not certain about my future, I am certain I'll never forget how fortunate I was to have been brought up by such a good and compassionate woman as my granny. Nor will I ever forget the kindness and understanding that the Sangha, the order of monks, gave to both of us when we needed it most, regardless of our reasons for needing it. To me, that shows the true compassion of Buddhism and of the monks in Thailand. In Buddhism, you shouldn't ask *why* people need help, or coldly assess the situation to decide whether someone is worthy of help or not – you just give whatever help you can when it's needed. That's what granny did for me when I was a child, and that's what the abbot of our monastery did for both of us. The teaching of the Buddha sustained my granny during the difficult times when she had to bring me up on her own. It helped me during the unhappy years when I lived with my aunt and cousins and it continues to sustain and guide both of us now. For all that, I give thanks to the Triple Gem: to the Buddha, the Dhamma and the Sangha.

An appeal from the Students' Education Trust

I n 1994, Phra Peter Pannapadipo and his friends established a small fund to help one impoverished Thai student study at university. More than enough was collected so the balance became the foundation of a non-profit-making charity dedicated to helping other students with similar difficulties. The charity – the Students' Education Trust – has since grown and now receives support from concerned people all around the world.

SET has a very specific aim: *to make a difference.* That difference is between a disadvantaged student being able to study at university or vocational college, or instead being forced to labour in the rice paddies, on a Bangkok building site, or in some other mundane, dead-end job.

More than 1,000 students have already benefited

from SET's Scholarship Programme. That's 1,000 university degrees or vocational diplomas for students who, without help, might never have been able to study at all. Hundreds more have benefited from SET's Student Welfare Programme, receiving grants to pay for their uniform and shoes, books and tools, bus fares or for school lunch. Through its Educational Projects Programme, SET sponsors English Language Camps, Narcotic Drugs' Awareness Camps and other projects with both short and long term benefits. The 'SET for Society' Programme encourages scholarship students to voluntarily work with orphans, handicapped children, AIDS patients and old people. Students also give thousands of hours of voluntary labour each year to renovate rural primary schools. Every year since 1994, SET has improved and expanded its programmes to reach increasing numbers of students. We do it voluntarily, cost-effectively and with great enthusiasm.

It costs very little to make a difference but there are thousands of students in Thailand who are prevented from achieving anything worthwhile simply because of their impoverished backgrounds. By supporting SET, you can make a positive difference to the lives of some of these deserving young men and women.

To find out more about SET and how you can help, please contact:

Peter S. Robinson, Director, The Students' Education
Trust, Academic Resource Centre, Rajabhat University,
Sawanwithi Road, Amphur Muang, Nakhon Sawan
60000, Thailand.

Email: SET_THAI@hotmail.com
Website: www.thaistudentcharity.org.

Phra Farang:
An English Monk in Thailand
Phra Peter Pannapadipo

At forty-five, successful businessman Peter Robinson gave up his comfortable life in London to ordain as a Buddhist monk in Bangkok. But the new path he had chosen was not always as easy or as straightforward as he hoped it would be.

In this truly extraordinary memoir, Phra Peter Pannapadipo describes his ten-year metamorphosis into a practising Buddhist monk, while being initiated into the intricacies of an unfamiliar Southeast Asian culture.

Phra Peter tells his story with compassion, humour and unflinching honesty. It's the story of a 'Phra Farang' – a foreign monk – living and practising his faith in an exotic and intriguing land.

arrow books

**Order further Arrow titles
from your local bookshop, or have them delivered
direct to your door by Bookpost**

☐ **Phra Farang** Phra Peter Pannapadipo 0099484471 £6.99

Free post and packing
Overseas customers allow £2 per paperback

Phone: 01624 677237

Post: Random House Books
c/o Bookpost, PO Box 29, Douglas, Isle of Man IM99 1BQ

Fax: 01624 670923

email: bookshop@enterprise.net

Cheques (payable to Bookpost) and credit cards accepted

Prices and availability subject to change without notice.
Allow 28 days for delivery.
When placing your order, please state if you do not wish to receive any
additional information.

www.randomhouse.co.uk/arrowbooks

THE POWER OF READING

Visit the Random House website and get connected with information on all our books and authors

EXTRACTS from our recently published books and selected backlist titles

COMPETITIONS AND PRIZE DRAWS Win signed books, audiobooks and more

AUTHOR EVENTS Find out which of our authors are on tour and where you can meet them

LATEST NEWS on bestsellers, awards and new publications

MINISITES with exclusive special features dedicated to our authors and their titles

READING GROUPS Reading guides, special features and all the information you need for your reading group

LISTEN to extracts from the latest audiobook publications

WATCH video clips of interviews and readings with our authors

RANDOM HOUSE INFORMATION including advice for writers, job vacancies and all your general queries answered

Come home to Random House

www.randomhouse.co.uk